MAMA
May I

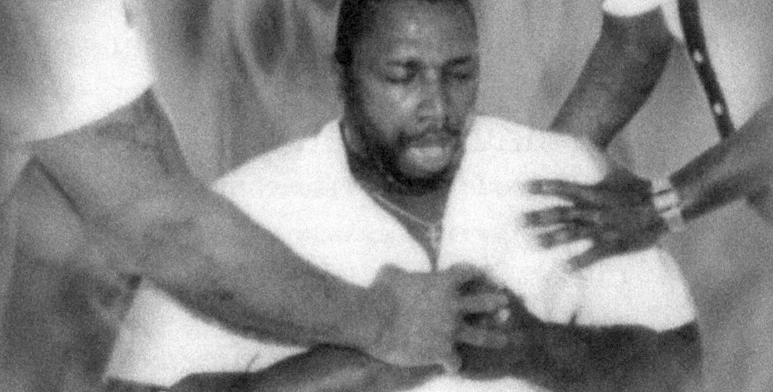

Dr. Charlotte Russell Johnson

Author of

A Journey to Hell and Back

A production of

Reaching Beyond, Inc.

www.charlotterjohnson.com

P. O. Box 12364

Columbus, GA 31917-2364

(706) 221-8572

Also available @ www.charlotterjohnson.com

It's Easier to Hide

It's easier to hide...
There's too much pain inside...
Some people call it pride...
The pain is eating me from inside...

Oh, that I might be free....
He keeps calling me...
My hidden pains, He can see...
Free! I would love to be...
Truth seems too hard for me...

It's easier to hide...
There's an emptiness inside...
In whom would I confide?
It's just easier to hide...
The hole keeps growing wide...
There is something that He wants from me...
Tell me what can it be?
What could He see in me?
Is it something that I can't see?
I can't trust me!
My failures surround me...

It's easier to hide...
My doubts won't subside...
It's not my pride...
It's just easier to hide...
Failure is where I reside...

Doesn't He Understand?
I see nothing in my hand...
Failure wasn't my plan...
Success isn't in this hand...
It's just easier to hide...
I never fail if I haven't tried...
It's much easier to hide!

Dedication

to

Henry "Buckwheat" Johnson

For all the things that you have brought into my life. I would not be who I am today without the lasting memories of the things that I have learned from our relationship. May you find true joy and wholeness!

In Memory
Of

"Dollie Mae Weldon"

June 5, 1923 - March 5, 2005

Hiding Places

Preface

This is my fifth book. In some ways, it has been the easiest to write. However, at the other end of the spectrum, it has been the most difficult and heart wrenching. In accepting the charge to write this book, I agonized in a way very similar to that I felt in writing the first book, *A Journey to Hell and Back*. On numerous occasions, I have been asked if the first book was therapeutic. That wasn't the purpose of that book. In writing *Mama May I,* however, I have found therapeutic release in dealing with a very painful and trying period in my life. Nonetheless, I remained shocked by the events that have transpired in my life in recent months.

Perhaps, some thought that I would be too embarrassed to write about them. I'm sure that they hoped many of these deeds would never see print. However, when deceit and treachery are done openly and notoriously, it's never really hidden. Therefore, I have chosen to share openly what some have discussed in private. This book has brought me a lot of personal and reflective growth. As always, I pray that you will be blessed by the honesty shared in this book.

As in my previous book, *Grace Under Fire*, this book will discuss some issues that may be sensitive or disturbing. There are some things that should not be named among the body of Christ. Those who engage in these acts are often mistakenly identified as Christians. Many of the events in this book were done openly and notoriously and then reported as sanctioned by God. In reading this book, please know that my intentions are not to embarrass anyone. Nevertheless, I intend to expose these deeds of darkness for what they are, an abomination to the body of Christ.

Each book has a unique message. The first book, *A Journey to Hell and Back* is an autobiographical account of my life. It details major events in my life, which almost destroyed me. However, these events were shared to provide hope and encouragement to others who had been beaten by the trials of life.

My second book, *Daddy's Hugs* exhorts the role of fathers in the lives of children. The book praises and provides examples of fathers who take a diligent role in parenting. It also portrays my appreciation of my husband, Henry Johnson.

My third book, *A Journey to Hell and Back: The Flip Side* tells both sides of the journey. The Flip Side is my husband's version of the events in our lives. We share our separate struggles, which became a common struggle. The book focuses on our different pasts that influenced our future.

In *Grace Under Fire*, I discussed unfavorable or controversial issues to the body of Christ. The church has been labeled as being full of hypocrites. There may be a measure of truth in this statement; hypocrites are everywhere. My husband was portrayed very accurately, although sometimes unflatteringly. The purpose of the book was not flattery. Actually, it discussed the dangers of a flattering woman.

In each of my previous books, my husband was referred to as Buck. However, in this book, I will refer to him as Henry. Although he is still manifesting some of the behaviors associated with Buck, my desire is to see him completely shake off his old nature. Therefore, I'm calling him Henry.

My prayer remains that lives will be enriched by something written in these books.

All scripture references are from the King James Bible unless otherwise noted.

Introduction by Earline Hall

Mama May I is the fifth book in author Charlotte Johnson's series of motivational texts. After twenty-two years of battling addiction and multiple incarcerations, the family appears to have reached a state of calm. This is merely the calm prior to the greatest storm this family has ever faced. Just as the family begins to deal with the effects of years of institutionalization and the residual effects of chronic drug use, a surprise visitor arrives in town throwing the family into chaos. After a family secret and conspiracy is revealed, the reader along with Ms. Johnson is forced to reevaluate everything they have previously known about the family. As the plot progresses, the layers of the conspiracy are subtly exposed revealing a depth of sin and deceit reminiscent of Nathaniel Hawthorne's *The Scarlet Letter*. Will the family be able to weather this storm?

This book reveals a level of honesty infrequently seen in authorized biographies and memoirs. Ms. Johnson is able to bring to life the effects of substance abuse on the user and the entire family system. She is able to acknowledge her codependent behavior and its effect on her children. Although hopeful that the family will be able to overcome its past now that Mr. Johnson in clean and sober, they soon realize that every action has a consequence. Can a man take fire into his bosom and not be burned?

Ms. Johnson explores how negative behavioral patterns can be learned and transmitted over multiple family generations and within a community. This is an excellent book for those living in or working with substance and alcohol abusing families, codependents, counselors, or those experiencing divorce, married or preparing for marriage, a member of an extended family, anyone recovering from betrayal, forced to reevaluate their life goals or in need of a great book.

The surprise ending will leave the reader questioning along with Ms. Johnson; "Can you ever really know someone?" One thing is very clear after reading this book. "All that glitters is not gold and every good-bye ain't gone." Once again, Ms. Johnson invites her readers to view her life as an open book and experience God's Grace and unmerited favor.

Ms. Doll

Who is a God like unto thee, that pardoneth iniquity, and passeth by the transgression of the remnant of His heritage? He retaineth not His anger forever, because He delighteth in mercy.
Micah 7:18

Ms. Doll was born on June 5, 1923, in Atlanta, GA. She later moved to Columbus, GA. She gave birth to five children, three sons, and two daughters. Michael was her youngest child. Henry was her fourth child. She was his first mother. I was to become his second mother. He was also her second son.

Ms. Doll was strong willed and determined. She was often headstrong and stubborn. By no stretch of the imagination would she be referred to as a weak woman. When Henry met me, he met a woman with many of the same characteristics or should I say character defects? Consciously, he may not have been aware of this fact. However, it didn't take much for Ms. Doll to recognize a kindred spirit. We were destined to clash.

On Mother's Day 1984, I met her for the first time. It was the day that I met most of Henry's extended family. We were both legally married to other people. Meeting his family should have been an uncomfortable situation but it wasn't. We had also formed a very deep an intimate attachment for each other. It was a very obvious attachment. The first meeting went off without any major complications.

Perhaps, Ms. Doll thought she would see her son regularly with his new move back to Columbus. This wasn't to be. Within days of his moving in with me, his drug addiction resurfaced full force. There was another problem that came with it. I had a major character defect. Since early childhood, my behavior had leaned towards co-dependency.

One night, Ms. Doll called our home. She had a message from Henry's wife. She asked him to call her. It was well after midnight when she called us. I answered the telephone and handed the telephone to him. He promised to call his wife. However, after he finished the conversation with his mother, he made no effort to make that second call. Ten minutes later, Ms. Doll called back.

Obviously irritated, she asked, "What are you doing?"

She blamed me for his failure to make the telephone call. After the second intrusion, he made a brief telephone call. This was the beginning of storms to come.

A couple of months later, Henry went to jail. This was related to the shoplifting charges that we had incurred together. In a later chapter, I'll provide further details of this encounter.

While Henry was serving his time, my role as his mother began to expand. At the time, Ms. Doll didn't resent this role. In fact, she praised me for my loyalty and devotion. Mama #2 made sure that he had everything he needed during his incarceration. This was going to be another consistent pattern in our relationship.

During Henry's incarceration, I was arrested again. My fear of serving a prison sentence led me to salvation or repentance. Henry's drug usage was no longer acceptable to me. He promised me that he would no longer abuse the drugs. When he was released from prison, he reneged on his promise. This changed things in our relationship.

Henry was no longer comfortable getting high around me. He needed a new playground. An addict's favorite place to get high is their playground. As it turned out, the playground was a back bedroom at his mother's house. His addiction pushed him to find a way to continue his drug usage. My compulsion pushed me to try to stop him.

Ms. Doll didn't understand our character defects. In the middle of the night, I would call her house asking to speak to Henry. She was often awake because a number of people were going in and out of the house.

She would respond, "No baby, I haven't seen him."

The night is far spent, the day is at hand: let us therefore cast off the works of darkness, and let us put on the armour of light. Let us walk honestly, as in the day; not in rioting and drunkenness, not in

chambering and wantonness,
not in strife and envying.
Romans 13:12-13

Eventually, I would make my way to her house. Rather than knocking on the front door, I went to the back yard. A light was usually on in the back bedroom. After waiting a few minutes to verify there was activity on the other side of the window, I knocked.

In a very firm voice, I demanded, "Henry, come out of there!"

His answer depended on how many drugs were left. If the drugs were gone, he would come with me. In the beginning if he had drugs left, he would ask me to give him a few minutes. As time went on, I was more determined to ruin his high. He was more determined not to go with me.

Ms. Doll couldn't understand why I was hindering her son from being at her home. She began to resent my unannounced visits. These visits were going to continue sporadically for a number of years.

When Henry told Ms. Doll that we were getting married, she was not impressed. She refused to come with us. Instead, she gave him a stern warning.

As if she was certain of the accuracy of her information, she proclaimed, "You better be careful of the hands that you eat from! All women believe in roots!"

It was rare that Henry challenged his mother but this was one of those rare occasions.

He retorted, almost jokingly, "Are you saying that you believe in roots, Mama?"

Although she initially wasn't happy about the marriage, when I went to jail the day after the marriage, Ms. Doll was one of my three visitors. During the second weekend of my incarceration, she came to the Muscogee County Jail to update me on my new husband.

She came straight to the point, "I don't know what's wrong with Henry Lee! I went to check on him. There was a woman there. I think she's living there. I wanted you to know it. I don't approve of what he's doing! I have nothing to do with it!"

Within a few days, Henry and the woman were locked up. Rumors traveled fast through the jail. Henry denied that there was any substance to the rumors. He insisted the woman was involved with one of his friends. When I was released from prison eleven months later, I discovered the truth of Ms. Doll's report. Henry was still serving his sentence.

Henry was serving his time in Columbus, Georgia. Each Saturday and every holiday, I went to see him. As I had done on his previous sentence, I tried to make him comfortable in an uncomfortable situation. From time to time, I also went to see Ms. Doll. We were learning how to tolerate each other.

One of Henry's uncles was a frequent guest at her house. They would tell me stories from their childhood. We would laugh for hours at their miraculous survival. Their childhood was filled with excitement and danger. Uncle Chase had endless tales. These were my favorites.

As if he could still see the scene, he said, "Doll was always a tattle tale. I was always trying to figure out a way to get even with her. We had a makeshift swing. I lifted her up in the basket. When she reached the top level, I let go of the rope and she landed on her bottom.

Once, our mother asked me to soak the peas. I added soap to them. As the peas were cooking, suds were going everywhere.

There was the time my brother and I acted like mules. We got all the children in the wagon. We got in front as if we were mules. We started down the hill. The wagon was going so fast that we jumped out of the way. The wagon wrecked but no one was hurt."

At this point, Ms. Doll would jump in, "What about the cats?"

Uncle Chase would continue, "I tied two cats together by their tails and hung them from the clothes line. One time, I tied two cats together by the tail and put paper between them. When I sat the paper on fire, you should have seen it. They were running around in circles."

Uncle Chase died a few years later. Ms. Doll and I often reminisced about his stories. We enjoyed our time together. That is until Henry was released from prison.

Whenever Henry was released, the trips to the back room at Ms. Doll's house started again. My late night trips to the back window started again. Eventually, this escalated. My frustration began to show. I started dropping his clothes off on his playground. This angered Ms. Doll and she called me terrible names.

Within a few days, my frustration would give way to fear. I was afraid Henry was going to overdose at his mother's house. Accompanied by apologies and tears, I would beg him to come home. He would make his own apologies and promises. We sincerely meant the things that we said. We just couldn't keep them.

Once, I went to Ms. Doll's looking for him. Everyone was silent. Two small boys pointed to the bedroom closet. There he was, hiding in the closet. Henry was high and was not ready to go home. We fought in Ms. Doll's front yard. It wasn't a knock down drag out fight but he did hit me. He also pulled my hair. He wasn't prone to hit me but he responded to my agitation. He later said that he wasn't trying to hurt me. The next day, he came home. I gave him the hair that had been pulled from my head as a souvenir.

It wasn't long after this that my relationship with Ms. Doll changed. As Henry continued to mount the number of his incarcerations, they sent him farther away from home. Ms. Doll began to express her appreciation for my determination to visit him.

On more than one occasion, she said, "I don't know how you do it! You get up (travel or go) and down that road to find Henry Lee. I just can't do it! I'm tired of going to those places. I wish my boys would stay out of those places. I'm so glad I'm no longer on Parkchester (referring to her old street address). The police stayed at that house looking for somebody."

If any man be in Christ, he is a
new creature: old things are
passed away; behold, all
things are become new.
2 Corinthians 5:17

After I finished college and received a pardon from the governor, I was concerned about my reputation. Public confrontations with Henry needed to stop. It was time for my late night trips to the drug neighborhoods and high-speed car chases to cease. There were times when I had the urge to look for him but I fought against that urge. He spent more time at Ms. Doll's house. She was able to observe the monster that I had been fighting against. She learned to love the things about me that had stirred hatred in the past. Our conversations changed. Our roles reversed. In the past, Ms. Doll encouraged me to give him some freedom. She even told me to let him have some fun at home. This was not an option. Those days were gone forever.

When he was abusing the drugs, I wanted him away from me. Before our first divorce, he moved in with Ms. Doll. The chains had been loosened. As a result, the addiction escalated. He was rapidly losing weight. Some family members said that they barely recognized him. Now that I was allowing him the space for his fun, Ms. Doll wanted me to keep a closer watch on him.

My dear Martha, . . . there is really

only one thing worth being concerned about.
Luke 10:41-42 NLT

This was not the worry of an overprotective mother. Ms. Doll knew firsthand the devastation of substance abuse. She also knew the realities of the streets. She had watched as drugs wreaked havoc in her family. Ms. Doll knew the signs, wakefulness and reduced hunger. She was also familiar with the psychological effects, which include feelings of wellbeing and a grandiose sense of power and ability, mixed with anxiety and restlessness. As the drugs wear off, these temporary sensations of mastery are replaced by an intense depression, and the drug abuser will then "crash", becoming lethargic and typically sleeping for several days.

With urgency in her voice, on more than one occasion, Ms. Doll begged, "Please go find my boy. I haven't seen him in several days. I'm worried about him. Get Darlene (her granddaughter) to ride with you!"

She didn't have to beg me. I was worried about him, too. Darlene was also worried about him. We would make a quick trip through his favorite neighborhoods. It never took long to find him. Rather than taking him to Ms. Doll's house, I brought him home. As if he were my child, I bathed him, fed him, and wrapped him in my arms. As long as he was with me, Ms. Doll wasn't worried. She was assured of his safety. No drugs were allowed in our home. In the earlier years, she had encouraged me to let him have fun at home. Now, she found comfort in knowing that I would no longer allow drugs near me. He wouldn't be having that type of fun at home.

Everything else is worthless when
compared with . . . knowing Christ.
Philippians 3:8 NLT

During the latter part of 1998, **I decided** that I couldn't take the cycle anymore. Rather than interceding, **I decided** to let Henry wallow with the pigs. **I was tired** of trying to make him give up the drugs. He seemed happy with his drug usage. **I was tired** of living with the fear and the drama. It seemed easy to walk away. Hindsight tells me this was unwise. It's true that I needed to stop rescuing him but this prolonged period of drug usage was extremely dangerous to his health.

For months, Henry indulged in his drug usage with very few interruptions. Each drug user has a different bottom. It is often necessary to hit the bottom, before looking up. It seemed to me that I was standing between Henry and the bottom. If I moved out of the way, just maybe, he would find a meaningful relationship with God. This seemed to be the right answer.

No matter what our choices are today, they are ultimately creating our future. Every choice that we make will either cause us to be blessed or cursed. Another way to put it is that things will get better or worse for us. All of our choices have consequences. These consequences will be for our betterment or will work to destroy us. We are also responsible for our choices.

"I call heaven and earth to record
this day against you, that I have set
before you life and death, blessing
and cursing: therefore choose life,
that both thou and thy seed may live"
Deuteronomy 30:19

Many messages going forth in our society today have stressed our "right to choose" but they haven't balanced it with the message that our choices also have consequences (especially in the area of lust and selfishness.) For example, most movies have glamorized many things that are harmful to us. Usually, they haven't shown the shattering results of drugs, smoking, drinking, adultery, fornication, gambling, abortion, etc.

These things don't often hit home until...

a. Someone we love gets cancer and is dying.
b. A drunken driver kills someone.
c. Family members divorce because of the unfaithfulness of a mate.
d. A friend or family member is infected with a sexually transmitted disease they will have for life.
e. A family loses their home because of gambling debts or drug usage.
f. A young person's life is destroyed because of drug usage.

After Henry had been hanging out in the streets for several months, I decided to end our marriage. When I decided to end my marriage to Henry, the love was still there. I loved him and I knew that he loved me. Love just didn't seem to be enough to sustain our relationship. We needed something stronger if the marriage was going to survive. It seemed to me that we didn't have what it was going to take for our marriage to endure. Rather than nagging Henry, I began nagging God. Rather than asking Him to deliver Henry, I was begging for permission to end our marriage.

It didn't matter that infidelity wasn't the reason that I was seeking a divorce. I couldn't prove that he had been unfaithful but we had shared many of our shortcomings. On more than one occasion, our wedding vows had been violated. You see we were also friends. Sometimes our secrets were difficult to keep. When it was all said and done, I really didn't have to worry about any woman taking my place in his life, and he definitely didn't have to worry about another man stealing my heart. The things that happened were part of the lifestyle, part of the drug culture. I only **wanted** one man, Henry Johnson. I stress "wanted" because there was a time when I believed that I needed him. It was no longer a need but a want. He had another mistress, drugs. They were his first love.

And now, brethren, I commend you
to God, and to the word of His
grace, which is able to build you up,

and to give you an inheritance among
all them which are sanctified.
Acts 20:32

Frustrated, I walked away from the man that I **Loved**. I decided to let God have him because I just couldn't handle any more. In the summer of 1999, I filed for a divorce. Shortly after filing for the divorce, I went to check on Henry. He was near his mother's old address. This was one of his favorite watering holes. Indeed, it was called "the hole". It had been several weeks since we had seen each other. When I drove up, he saw me. He walked over to the car and we had a brief conversation. He came home with me and we sat on the front porch.

This was a new experience. As always, I went into rescue mode. However, I was able to constrain my feelings for him. I brought him food to eat and we talked. We had both missed spending time together. However, I didn't allow him to come inside the house. During the visit, I never looked in his eyes. That would have been dangerous. The pain there would have been unbearable. If I looked into his eyes, the cycle would start again. Before I gave in to the feelings, I drove him back to the place where I had found him. A few days later, he was in jail.

Jesus said: "Have you not read...that
at the beginning the Creator made
them male and female," and said:
'For this reason a man will leave his

father and mother and be united to
His wife, and the two will become
one flesh?' "So, they are no longer
two but one. Therefore, what
God has joined together,
let man not separate."
Matthew 19: 4-6 NIV

Before the divorce was final, he began serving his fifth prison sentence since our relationship began. It was his eighth adult conviction. After I left the courtroom finalizing our first divorce, a strange thing happened. I had overwhelming sense of being married; Ms. Russell was my mother, not me. I was Charlotte Johnson, not Charlotte Russell or Charlotte Russell Johnson. A person may be able to physically separate the husband and wife from each other but not the marriage or "oneness" that they possess in their hearts. The "oneness" was still intact. The night we became one was not doing a wedding ceremony. This occurred several years after our marriage ceremony. The chemistry between us was often overwhelming and seemed miraculous.

"Comfort, comfort My people,"
says your God.
Isaiah 40:1 NLT

Henry was incarcerated from the summer of 1999 until October 2003. Two major events happened in Ms. Doll's life during this time. The first crisis was the death of her second husband, Mr. John. We had been divorced for some time. As usual, I knew that Henry needed me. The divorce wasn't going to keep me from supporting him. I visited him in prison and filled in for him with Ms. Doll. The kids and I spent a great deal of time with her. During one of my visits, it got kind of touchy. My sister-in-law Marjorie was there. She was always prone to speak her mind. This occasion would be no different.

When she could hold her thoughts no longer, she shared them with me, "You need to send your husband some money!"

To aggravate her, I responded, "I don't have one."

Very few people knew we were divorced on paper. It was on paper only. In our hearts, we were very much married.

Marjorie responded angrily, "I never wanted you to be my sister-in-law."

He that keepeth his mouth keepeth
his life: but he that openeth wide his
lips shall have destruction.
Proverbs 13:3

Marjorie said this more out of temporary anger. Over the years, she and I had our differences. It had never been anything major. To my knowledge, she had never allowed Henry to get high at her home. Since our marriage, she had never encouraged his involvement with another woman. My statement also shocked Ms. Doll.

With a puzzled look on her face, she acknowledged, "Henry Lee told me some mess like that but I didn't believe it. He said you sent the papers to the jail."

That was the end of the conversation. A few days later, Marjorie called me. She wanted to ride with me to see Henry. The next morning, I picked her up at her home. There were a few rules that needed to be in place before we left. My car is a drug-free environment. This includes alcohol and cigarettes.

Marjorie has a very vivid imagination. As we drove for almost three hours to reach the prison, she entertained me with a number of stories.

Henry's younger brother, Michael was also incarcerated at the prison where Henry was serving time. Normally, siblings weren't allowed to be incarcerated at the same facility. This had to be the mercy and grace of God. It gave them time to mend their relationship. Mike had issues with Henry. This also gave me an opportunity to witness to him. Mike had begun studying with one of the groups in the prison. I sent him some information exposing the inaccuracies of their teachings.

When Marjorie and I arrived at the prison, we requested special permission for Mike to be allowed to visit with us. We didn't know that Henry and Mike were attempting to conceal their relationship from the prison officials. They were concerned that this knowledge would result in one of them being shipped to another camp. The officers agreed to let them sit at adjacent tables. Both brothers were shocked when they arrived at visitation. It had been years since we had seen Mike.

We were able to purchase snacks from a machine. Henry's appetite was still enormous. He ate Buffalo wings, cheeseburgers, fish sandwiches, chips, and dessert. On the other hand, Mike's appetite was quite different. He ate honey buns and drank sodas. Marjorie talked between both tables. She told one story after another. She kept both of her brothers laughing. However, she must have told Mike something extra. He was roaring with laughter. I had never seen him have so much fun.

After the visit was over, Marjorie and I drove back to Columbus. On the way back, she talked about my rules and me. This made me laugh. She was anxious to tell Ms. Doll about this and our visit.

Ms. Doll was so glad that we had seen her sons. She had a special relationship with her youngest son. She also had a special love and concern for Mike. She was waiting for the day he would be released from prison. Mike didn't tell his mother how long his sentence was.

Ms. Doll reminisced, "I'll be so glad when Mike comes home. He can help me around the house. He will fix things for me. He's not like Henry Lee; he doesn't like to get his hands dirty. I don't have to worry about Henry because he has you. I just wish Mike would find a nice girl. I wish my boys would stay out of that place. They aren't like Junior. I just hope this will be their last time. I want them to come home and stay."

When Henry's sister Annie heard about the

visit Marjorie and I took, she wanted to visit her brothers. I made plans for Annie to travel with me on my next trip. She lives approximately twenty miles from Columbus. It was raining hard the night Earline and I drove to Alabama to pick her up. Annie spent the night with Ms. Doll. The next day, we made the trip to the prison. God was merciful, and the brothers were allowed to sit at the same table. They were housed in different dorms and seldom got a chance to interact. At the time, we didn't know how special these visits would later become.

Occasionally, I would visit Henry at the prison. There were times when my need to see him was overpowering. Nevertheless, I was determined not to continue enabling him. Except for an occasional letter or money order, he needed to complete this bid on his own. I hoped that if I stayed out of the way, God would become the source of his strength. Just maybe, he would learn the things that he needed to break this cycle. During each of his previous incarcerations, I had begged God to send him home. I had also begged the parole board, by writing countless letters. Once, I took several people from our church to the parole board with me to intercede for him.

And he said if now I have found
grace in Thy sight, O Lord, let my
Lord, I pray Thee, go among us; for
it is a stiffnecked people; and
pardon our iniquity and our sin, and

take us for Thine inheritance.
Exodus 34:9

This time, I was analyzing my behavior. Maybe, I was the problem. When you are in a race, you don't finish it until you cross the finish line. The same happens with a test. If you stop before the test is over, you haven't completed the test. If you ever hope to complete the race or the test, you don't get the option of starting where you left off. You have to start at the beginning. I loved him enough to move out of the way. This time, I was praying for Henry, however, it was a different prayer.

Finishing is better than starting.
Patience is better than pride.
Ecclesiastes 7:8 NLT

Whenever I thought of him, I prayed, "Lord let my husband learn the things that he needs to know from this incarceration, so he won't keep starting over."

Although I explained this to Henry, this wasn't what he wanted to hear. Henry and I eventually had a disagreement. My visits were discontinued again. Several months passed and we had no contact.

One day, Henry called me, his brother, Michael was terminally ill. The news was shocking; our visit didn't seem that long ago. There was no talk of love. This was a short phone call, an almost casual conversation between distant friends.

Mike's health was declining rapidly. He went to the state hospital several times for tests. The last time, he went for an operation. After the operation was over, an infection set in.

On November 23, 2002, Ms. Doll's second tragedy struck. Earlier in the week, I had written Henry. I informed him that I might come for a visit on the upcoming Sunday. That Saturday night, I was driving back to Columbus. Henry's sister, Annie called me. Michael had died that morning.

The next day, I went to see Henry. Annie rode with me. When we arrived at the prison, I couldn't believe I was there. When he walked into the room and our eyes met, I knew our feelings were still alive. During the visit, I massaged his hands and looked into his eyes. For almost five hours, I stared at him. There was very little said between us. What was there to say? As he talked with his sister, I watched him. I watched his pain. My heart was filled with compassion for him. In my heart, I knew God wanted me there with him. This was not in my plan. My plans were for a new relationship, with someone new.

When we left him, my eyes were strained from staring at him. It was shocking to discover that I was still in love with him. It was as if time had stood still. I thought that we had both moved on. There were no right words to say to help his grief. Additionally if we started talking to each other, we might forget Annie was there. We were both conscious of her presence. Normally, I visited him alone. Our time and conversations were special.

We had been doing it that way so long that we were both uncomfortable having someone else at the table.

I will heal their backsliding, I will love them freely: for mine anger is turned away from him.
Hosea 14:4

God restored our relationship; yet, He gave me a new love for Henry. He gave me an appreciation for him that I didn't have before. Through my hurt and pain, I had been focused on the negatives in our relationship. God used Michael's death to help us put aside our petty differences.

As I had done with the passing of Mr. John, I filled in for Henry, again. This time, it went a little deeper. This crisis took finances. On Henry's behalf, I made the contribution.

Henry took his brother's death hard. During his previous incarcerations, a number of loved ones had passed. This one was different. It was what the brothers had feared, one of them dying in prison. It was the one thing they said that they didn't want to happen. Mike had died in prison. It hit close to home. It could have been Henry. His life could have ended behind bars. Michael's death made Henry determined not to go back to prison. One of them needed to break this cycle.

Several people we knew had become seriously ill while in prison. Henry had watched them deteriorating. They were dying away from home and their families. This was a fate no inmate wanted to suffer. Some inmates were given a reprieve to return home. Mike died before his reprieve was granted.

Ms. Doll was really shaken by the loss of her youngest child. She said that she wouldn't be able to attend Mike's funeral. She worried that she would never see her other son, Henry. As always, his other mama stepped in. Arrangements were made for Henry to come to the funeral. This was a difficult task since Henry had two escapes on his prison record. He relied on my ability to fix any situation. He was sure that I would work it out and he wasn't disappointed. Since Ms. Doll wasn't attending the funeral, I needed to find a way for her to see Henry. I worked this out as well.

Marjorie also took Mike's death hard. She ordered a tape on depression. After listening to the tape several times, she brought it to Ms. Doll. After the tape played for about ten minutes, Ms. Doll verbalized my thoughts.

Turning to me, she said, "That mess is making me depressed."

Truthfully, I think the tape did more to depress Marjorie than it did to help. Each death is unique and therefore each person's experience is unique. Indeed some of the advice available becomes contradictory simply because each person must deal with their own grief in their own way. Grief is often seen as a process. It is long lasting and does not follow a fixed pattern. Grief has also been termed "work." People must "work-through" their own grief. Anyone who has been through grief will agree that it is indeed "hard work." Grief hurts. When we refer to the pain of grief, that pain is very real. Grief is a deep hurt. Just as one must heal from physical wounds, we must also heal from the emotional and psychological wound known as grief.

Depression is a normal emotion. Depression over a period of weeks or months with no signs of improvement is an abnormal behavior. Imagining seeing or hearing a deceased loved one is also normal. If these occurrences continue and become consuming, this is abnormal. Somehow, most people find a way to survive, and eventually overcome their grief and to thrive again.

During this time of grief, we spent a lot of time with Ms. Doll. Herman (my son by birth, (Henry's by choice) was already prone to spend the night with her whenever he had the notion. He and Ms. Doll would watch television together. They liked the same boring shows, cooking, ice skating, and fishing. She also liked cowboy pictures. There were several movies that she liked to watch repeatedly, *What About Bob, The Temptations, and The Five*

Heartbeats. We watched them so much that I became fond of them.

When Henry was released from prison on October 1, 2003, we were remarried. Ms. Doll told me to keep him at home with me. She wanted to see him but she no longer wanted him hanging out at her house. After Henry had been home a few months, my mother told him to make sure that he called his mother every day. This concerned me. Mama wouldn't share the reason for her encouragement with me. I had my suspicions but I didn't share them with Henry. Every day, Mama reminded Henry to call his mother.

When a major change occurs, people have similar reactions of fear, anxiety, self-doubt, and a lack of control. The difference occurs in how individuals respond to the change. In June of 2004, our house caught fire. This experience was emotionally draining for me. My marriage to Henry crumbled under the weight of the pressure that I was under. In many ways, I felt he wasn't offering me enough emotional support. He had his own set of complaints. Our arguments became more heated and more frequent. I was tired of the arguments and the lack of communication between us. Arguments don't facilitate communication.

Dear brothers and sisters, be quick to listen, slow to speak, and slow to get angry. Your anger can never make things right in God's sight.
James 1:19-20 NLT

Henry moved back in with Ms. Doll. He received a big nudge from me. I rushed to get a second divorce. This was the second time that I had divorced Henry without God's approval. There is a major difference between us doing something from our own determination and carrying out the loving will of our heavenly Father.

God is deeply grieved when He sees marriages unravel but we know that He loves us and is willing to forgive us and help us mend our shattered lives. Although it was another messy situation, I believed that Henry needed to spend time with his mother. This was sober time spent with her. This was something that she hadn't experienced very often since he was an adolescent. Between 1973 and 2003, Henry wasted approximately twenty years incarcerated. During these years, Ms. Doll seldom saw him. He returned home on October 1, 2003. We were married for the second time that day. We separated on July 18, 2004. Our second divorce was final on August 13, 2004.

A month after the divorce, I was no longer angry with Henry. He had resolved not to come near me. He was also seeing someone else, Sister Juanita. I was determined to restore our marriage relationship. After a battle with depression, I began a battle to restore our marriage. Since he wouldn't talk to me, I wrote him a letter. This was the kind that he was all too familiar with. It was a love letter. Over the years, I had written him lots of letters. This one was one of my masterpieces! It's one that I'm sure he will never forget. He didn't respond to the letter, or should I say, he didn't contact me. I'm sure the letter is still deriving a response from him. Then I called the saints to pray. When the saints began to pray, things had to change.

When I began my campaign to restore the marriage, I spent several days with Ms. Doll. We watched her favorite videos and DVDs. Henry wasn't there. He was in Alabama with Sister Juanita. Ms. Doll prepared breakfast and I cooked dinner. We laughed about my crazy relationship with her son. She told me that he had gotten my letter. I was sure that he hadn't allowed her to read it. A few weeks later, on October 21, 2004, Henry and I married for the third time.

His sister Marjorie had often commented, "Anybody who would marry somebody three times must be in love."

At the time she said this, we had only been married twice. We had renewed our vows once. This was why she said it was three times. When we got married for the third time, I said it was Marjorie's fault.

On Saturday, March 5, 2005, I went to a small town in Alabama for a book signing. As I crossed the state line, my cell phone lost reception. There were no towers in the area. After about an hour, I became really uncomfortable being out of range. I left the signing early and headed back to Columbus.

Henry was working nearby. I decided to stop to check on him. After this, I continued on to the expressway. Approximately fifteen minutes down the road, I received a telephone call. It was my sister-in-law, Annie. Ms. Doll had passed. They had been unable to reach us. I called and left a message for Henry to meet me in Columbus. Additionally, I called Earline and Herman. I asked both of them to let me relay this information to Henry. However, Herman has his own ideas about everything. He got a second message to Henry. Rather than coming where I was, he went to see Herman. It was thus that he learned Mama #1 was gone.

And Isaac brought her into his mother Sarah's tent, and took Rebekah, and she became his wife; and he loved her: and Isaac was comforted after his mother's death.

Genesis 24:67

As we were prone to do in any crisis, we put aside our petty differences. As Rebekah comforted Isaac at the death of Sarah, Henry found comfort in my arms.

Never Neverland

How can a young person stay pure? By obeying Your word and following its rules.
Psalm 119:9 NLT

It is often said, "I would never do that. I don't know how you could do that. I can't believe this. I can't believe that." We have to be careful of the words that we speak. They are often repeated back to us. Actually, our words are often based on a lack of compassion or understanding. Sometimes, we believe we are immune to certain tendencies or behaviors. We may even believe that we are infallible.

When I began selling heroin in the late seventies, my cousin warned me never to become involved with a drug addict. Nevertheless, this cousin later became involved with a drug addict. It went a step further. The same cousin became a drug addict. The person that was supplying drugs for me to sell also became a drug addict. Moreover, I promised myself that I would never become involved with an addict. Never say never! That may very well be your next experience.

As children, my uncle and I watched firsthand the devastating effects of alcoholism. We were often taunted and humiliated by children in our neighborhood. On more than one occasion, I cried in frustration. There was nothing that we could do to help. When I was sixteen, I watched the devastating effects that drugs had on my uncle, Carlton.

Even during my early days of drug dealing, I saw many young people take their first injection of heroin. I befriended more than one addict. Big Liz was an addict that worked with me. In exchange for a small portion of the profits, she made most of the direct drug sales. Most of her profits circled back to me. Each day, we tried to make enough sales to enable her to rent a hotel room. No matter how good our sales were, usually Big Liz was short of funds. On the nights when I wasn't meeting Jim at one of the nightclubs on West Peachtree Street or Bankhead Highway, I rented a double room. This gave Big Liz a place to sleep. Jim (the guy I was involved with) suspected that I was feeling sorry for her but he didn't know about this arrangement. Although he wanted her to help me with selling the drugs, he didn't want me to become comfortable with her drug usage. There were a lot of young girls on the streets who were quickly being introduced to drug usage. They were quickly becoming addicted to heroin.

Big Liz was also pregnant. She refused to seek prenatal care because of her addiction. When Big Liz went into labor, she was more than a little hesitant to go to the hospital. If it was at all possible, she increased the frequency and the amount of heroin that she injected. After more than twenty-four hours of begging her

+let me take her to the hospital, I drove her there against her wishes. We were both scared. She was afraid of detoxing. We were both reluctant to be questioned about the drugs. After dropping her off, I made a speedy exit.

The next day, I went back to the hospital to check on the baby. The sight of that small baby in the high-risk nursery with tubes attached to his head should have been enough to scare me away from the drug scene. It wasn't.

The baby was blessed. He was a full term baby. Heroin babies experience growth restriction and premature birth. Only half of the babies born addicted to heroin are born alive. After delivery, babies who are exposed to heroin or methadone before they are born are likely to experience withdrawals. This was the fate of Big Liz's baby. The baby stayed in the hospital several weeks before being released. I'm not sure what happened to the baby after he left the hospital.

When I went to New York City a few years later, I saw drug addicts on a different level. This definitely should have put the fear of God in me. It did to a point. I was afraid to try the drugs. However, I was not ready to stop selling the drugs. In New York City, Jim became addicted to freebasing cocaine. Without my consent, Neverland became a reality. I was involved with an addict. I was not happy about this reality. In recent days, I have questioned how I came to this juncture in my life. Perhaps this is what eased me into the next step, **choosing** to become involved with an addict.

When Jim began freebasing, it changed our relationship forever. Although there was periodic involvement, I lost a measure of respect for him. He crossed the never ever line. He was determined however that I would never see him getting high. It went against everything that he had taught me about the drug scene. Our relationship had always been strange and it became stranger. During our previous interactions, we seldom spent prolonged time together. His addiction made it worse. He didn't want me to know that he had crossed the line.

The first time that I saw Henry, he was coming to my friend's house to get high. He was good looking and fine. At least, I thought so. From the beginning, I knew he had a problem with drugs. He wasn't the first handsome addict that I had met. He wasn't the best-looking one that I had met. He was, however, the only one that I ever felt attracted to. As it happened, untimely circumstances led to me crossing the boundary. It happened on a night when I was vulnerable and hurting. My defenses were down. I just wanted the pain to go away. I found comfort for my pain in Henry's arms. I found comfort in the arms of an addict.

There were no fireworks that night. It would have been easy to just walk away. It was special because it was out of my character. Perhaps, I was just desperate to get over Jim. For whatever reason, I decided to see him again. I was caught up in Never Neverland. If it had been another day or time in my life, maybe it wouldn't have happened.

Do or Don't

Everywhere we go, we tell everyone about Christ. We warn them and teach them with all the wisdom God has given us.
Colossians 1:28 NLT

In addition to the warnings that I received about all addicts, I received specific warnings about becoming involved with Henry 'Buckwheat' Johnson. They started the day after I met him. On more than one occasion, I was told, "He's a nice guy but he's going to stay in prison. Don't get involved with him unless you're prepared for that." His friends had also given him several nicknames, *Mad Scientist, Six-Year Man, Institutionalized, Buckwheat,* and *Henry Lee.*

He was called a *Mad Scientist* because he experimented with a variety of drugs and he didn't know when enough was enough. He showed no respect for the danger of the drugs. He mixed the drugs as if he had received formal training. Perhaps he did, street training.

He was dubbed a *Six-year Man* because all his sentences were six-year sentences. At least, that was the way it was reported. They also said he had already been to prison six times. They may have included juvenile convictions. At any rate, his friends were convinced that Henry was institutionalized.

The things that they told me about him made him more of a challenge. There were so many people who had counted him out that I was determined to help him succeed. The things that they said about him brought back painful memories of another drug, alcohol. Additionally, I understood having your name scandalized.

Jim gave me a different warning about Henry. He was obviously not fond of him. I don't know if this was related to my relationship with Henry or something that existed from times past. He never formally verbalized the reason for his low opinion. It was more in the tone of his voice when he spoke about him. When Jim learned about my involvement with Henry, he made an instant prediction.

With the voice of certainty, he said, "He's going to blow it. The nigga will take you for granted. He doesn't know what he has. I know and I know what it's like to take you for granted. He'll blow it, and when he does, I'll be waiting."

Jim maintained this conviction until his death. There were many times that I thought about his words. They often hit close to the truth. However, I wasn't going to let him know that he had been correct in his predictions.

Perhaps, the things that were said about him drew me closer to him. My first husband, Robert is an alcoholic. Yet, I never attempted to change him. I was disgusted and repulsed by his alcoholic behavior. I prayed for him but I never invested in his recovery.

During my relationship with Jim, I never saw

him smoke cocaine or crack. He made sure that never happened. There were times when I saw him under the influence. These times were few and far between. It was usually because I popped up unexpectedly. It wasn't a secret that he smoked. This was just another thing that he kept a safe distance from me.

Although I helped Jim sell the drugs, I was never present when he purchased the drugs or when he paid for them. He often told me where they came from but I never asked any questions. When he was plotting and scheming, he never told me about it until after it was over. Usually, I knew he was up to something that wasn't quite right. My eyes told him that I didn't like it.

With guilt in his eyes, he would say, "Charlotte Hall, don't start that mess. Stop looking at me like that."

If there were other people present, he grabbed me as if to restrain me. It was actually a hug or an embrace. When he was confident that I had gotten the message, he continued with his plot. Over the years, I heard many things about him. They weren't the types of things that I was told about Henry. He was called *A Low Down Nigga*. This meant he fit in perfectly with the street life. He was always looking for a way to get over on you. It was nothing personal. Friends just became part of his plots without their permission. Sometimes, he would correct the wrong at a later date, the later…the better.

Jim wanted me to respect him. Because I knew this was a priority, I never disrespected him.

After I became a Christian, I witnessed to him about God's goodness. There were many things about his behavior that I disliked but I made no investment in his recovery. When I could no longer tolerate his behavior, I excused myself from his company. Sometimes it was for a day, a week, or even years.

The views of co-dependency are as varied as the symptoms. While I haven't exhibited all of the symptoms, I would still label my behavior in many instances as that of a codependent personality. Almost from the beginning, I believed that if I did the right things, Henry would change his behavior. I wanted to counter all the negative things that I heard about him. I constantly flattered him. I told him how good he looked. He heard a different set of names from me. When I looked at him, I saw undeveloped potential. I was determined to promote and encourage his growth. With the proper support, he could change. At least, that's what I wanted to believe.

Over the years, I have attended a number of AA/NA meetings with Henry. There were those who insisted that I also have a substance abuse diagnosis because of my use of marijuana and cocaine over the years. There may be some truth to this assumption. However, my body never experienced withdrawals. I never craved the drugs as much as I did Henry Johnson. Therefore, I'll proceed with my primary problem, an almost unnatural attachment to the person who later became my husband.

For therein is the righteousness of God revealed from faith to faith: as

it is written, The just
shall live by faith.
Romans 1:17

In many ways, I took responsibility for his addiction. He was addicted years before I met him. Yet, at times, my sole purpose in life was to rescue him. I saw potential in him that he didn't see in himself. My faith said one day he would be drug-free. This attachment caused me to function in many instances as his mother rather than his wife. Even after I identified the behavior, it hindered my ability to function as his wife. In many ways, it also thwarted his attempts to treat me as a wife. He became too dependent on me.

Codependents are individuals who are reliant on an addict's dependency on a mind-altering substance or activity (e.g., alcohol, drugs, gambling, and sex.) The addict's dysfunctional behavior and the family's adaptation to it dictate and sustain the relationship between the addict and the codependent. The codependent plays a vital role in sustaining the relationship regardless of how destructive, loathsome or dysfunctional it is. The term, "enabling" is often used to describe this phenomenon. This refers to the codependent's role in preventing an addict from assuming responsibility for their behavior, life, and future.

You know these things so well that
you are able to teach others.
Romans 15:14 NLT

The codependent delays and blocks the necessary conditions that would likely lead the addict to seek help on their own. These conditions might include facing legal or criminal consequences for their conduct, being fired from a job or losing a meaningful relationship. The codependent's efforts to help the addict by protecting, intervening and excusing their conduct are unproductive in correcting or changing the addict's behavior.

Many therapists believe that co-dependency is a learned behavior that can be passed from one generation to the next. However, it may be a generational curse. This is an emotional and behavioral condition that affects an individual's ability to have healthy and mutually fulfilling relationships. Codependent behavior is learned by observing and imitating other family members who display this type of behavior. This is also termed "relationship addiction" because people with codependency often form or maintain relationships with addicts that are one-sided, emotionally destructive and abusive.

While irritated by my original behavior, Henry learned to enjoy the personal benefits of my conduct. He grew to expect certain things as a right or a privilege. There were countless calls to bondsmen, lawyers, wardens, judges, the parole board, parole officers, and probation officers. Who can offer a reasonable guess of the number of letters that I wrote over the years to keep him connected to home? I can't.

One of these letters was written on napkins. It was after one of my numerous trips to visit him in prison. On the way home, I stopped at a restaurant.

There was something that had upset me. It couldn't wait until I got home. I felt inspired. It took approximately eight full-size napkins to finish the letter. I dropped it in the first mailbox that I passed.

[God] will supply all your needs from
His glorious riches, which have been
given to us in Christ Jesus.
Philippians 4:19 NLT

For many years, my life was revolved around his convictions. I placed little value on my own needs and instead assumed responsibility for Henry's needs. It was important for him to be comfortable in prison. It was important for him to be released as soon as possible. When he returned home, it needed to be a seamless transition. He was never to wear prison clothes home. He was never to ride the bus home from prison. Once he returned home, he was not to wear outdated clothes. Like all good mothers, my child had very few problems that I didn't try to fix. Actually, I fixed most of them.

While he was serving time, I tried to make him comfortable in prison. I did his time with him. I made regular weekly visits to the prisons, wrote countless letters to him and the parole board, sent money orders, and packages. Rather than allowing God to have free course in Henry's life, I kept begging God to lighten the punishment. I was unwilling to let him endure his just punishment, which may have been God's way of drawing him nearer to Him. He needed to spend time with God. He needed to learn how to trust Him.

For do I now persuade men, or God?
or do I seek to please men? For if
I yet pleased men, I should not
Be the servant of Christ.
Galatians 1:10

During his last incarceration, I withheld some of the amenities that I usually provided for him. Nevertheless, I knew that upon his release, he would have difficulty finding a job making a legal livable wage. Each time he returned home, I tried to make his transition back into society painless. I rushed in to fix that problem, too. I had crippled him as much as the prison system. It was time to remove the crutches. If he would attempt to walk on his own, I was willing to help him. I wasn't willing to carry him or drag him.

Frequently, codependents are viewed as overcommitted, stressed, and pressured. They feel safe when giving. They have been victims of abandonment, alcoholism, sexual, physical, or emotional abuse, or neglect. Most codependents repress their own needs and desires. Their lives revolve around someone else's life. They tolerate abuse and feel trapped.

We may leave one bad relationship and jump into another one. I am admittedly guilty of this one. If it were possible, there are many of my previous relationships that I would erase. Codependents wonder if they will ever find true love. They allow others to hurt them, over and over again. They stay in bad relationships for all the wrong reasons: to fix the other person. Can we ever really fix someone else?

On more than one occasion, I have sincerely questioned my relationship with Henry Johnson. Was the relationship based on pity? Was it sympathy? Was it jealousy? Was it based on need? Was it my desire to never be defeated or give up on anything? Was it my hidden desire to self-destruct? Was it possessiveness? Was it loyalty? Did I really see something in him that no one else saw? Was there something redeemable in him? Was I delusional? Was this really love? Was it lust? Was it loneliness? Sad to say, at some time in our relationship, I have felt all of these things. Is that good or bad? It's honest.

Children living with an addict often develop behavior and personality patterns that have long-term effects on their lives. These children have difficulty communicating and trusting others. This can result in frequent physical complaints, low self-esteem, acting-out behavior, and isolation. The children may suffer ridicule or taunting in school and in the community. Without help, these children continue to develop problems at home and school. Frequently, the child's problems are not recognized as being related to the family's problem of addiction. The parents may be unaware of the source of the child's problem.

When I returned home from prison, it was obvious that Earline had some serious issues with me. She treated me as if I was a stranger. Earline preferred the company of her grandmothers. This confused me. I had no idea how to reach her. To complicate the problem, I was learning to cope with life outside of the prison. My life was in desperate need of repair. I had more responsibilities than I had time or money. I focused on getting a car and getting us a place to live, instead of becoming preoccupied with the things going on with Earline.

Characteristic of Co-dependency

- **They overcompensate**
- **They protect at all costs**
- **They second guess their own actions and often override common sense**
- **They have difficulties making decisions**
- **They struggle for control**
- **They live in a constant state of denial**
- **They make unreasonable compromises that seriously impact their lives, their happiness, and even their safety**
- **They remain committed to the addict in spite of their inability to do the same**
- **They maintain an unrealistic view that if "they" do the right things, their "addict" partner will change their behavior**
- **They place little value on their own needs and instead assume responsibility for those of the addict**
- **They are vulnerable to the addict's manipulation, a major impediment to healing and change**

Characteristics of an Addict:

- They lack empathy toward others
- They have a narrow range of emotions (usually limited to anger/rage and elation)
- They tend to communicate on a superficial level finding it difficult to discuss their feelings
- They live in a constant state of denial
- They are unwilling to accept responsibility for their behavior and recovery
- They project their own inadequacies on others and blame others for their problems
- They are unable to keep promises or commitments
- Albeit dysfunctional, their addiction is their method of coping with life's stresses
- They are highly manipulative

Addiction Understated!

O that they were wise, that they understood this, that they would consider their latter end!
Deuteronomy 32:29

The first drug that we battled against was heroin. Although Henry used a combination of other drugs during his heroin addiction, heroin was the driving force. Heroin is considered a depressant, a drug that slows the metabolism, breathing and heart rate down. Some heroin effects include an intense high, especially when injected. This is followed by a low that often makes the user quite sleepy or nod off. Heroin use can result in overdosing, meaning the heart and breathing stops and the heroin user dies unless someone acts fast to medically revive the person. Other heroin effects may also include hallucinations and a dream-like reality about life.

The heroin addict sees life as more of a mixture of thoughts and reality. This is called escape. When facts become too difficult to confront, heroin use produces a different reality for the user. Some drug users trying heroin for the first time became heroin addicts the same day.

Once they are addicted, the addict's primary purpose in life becomes seeking and using drugs. For Henry, this was no different. Once the addiction begins, the addict must use greater quantities of heroin to achieve the same intensity or effect. As higher doses are used over time, physical dependence and addiction develop. With physical dependence, the body has adapted to the presence of the drug and withdrawal symptoms may occur if the drug usage is reduced or stop.

When I decided that I was tired of a drug-induced lifestyle, I began a campaign to make Henry stop using the drugs. There were times when I threw his drugs away. There were other times when I tried to knock the works (needle) out of his hands. I became adept at blowing his high.

One day in an act of desperation, I tested him. Although he assured me that he loved me more than the drugs, I doubted this. He said that he loved me 'more than a hog loves slop.' We were at home sitting in the living room. Henry had tried repeatedly to find a good vein in his arms or legs. His repeated usage had caused many of his veins to collapse. He became a determined an expert marksman. As he repeatedly stuck himself, I became disgusted. My staring at him was probably contributing to the problem. When I could hold my disgust no longer, I began a tirade.

Determined to show how severe the problem was, I said, "Before you take another hit, hit me!"

Henry looked at me in shock and disbelief. He knew how I felt about the drugs. He was afraid that this was a trap. It was. After repeatedly questioning my sincerity, he relented. He tied a noose around my arm. My veins are small and difficult to find. This always presents a problem when having my blood drawn. Nevertheless, Henry quickly located one. He was so determined to get it over with so that he could finish his mission; it was difficult for him to hear me when I began to scream.

Repeatedly, I screamed, "You better not stick that mess in my arm!"

When he realized what I had done, he looked up with tears in his eyes. He was sorry but not sorry enough to throw the drugs away. I have never tried shooting drugs. This may have been the last time that he got high in my presence.

Addiction consumes the addict's mind, body, and soul as well as that of those who care for them. An addict's path of destruction is multidimensional as it affects family, friends and co-workers and is transmitted across generations. Even though many addicts may regret their behavior or the distress it causes family members, addicts believe that they are powerless to the effects of their addiction.

Withdrawing from heroin is a fact that all heroin addicts must face sooner or later. Some addicts believe that they can quit at any time. This was Henry's resolve. He quit often and relapsed frequently. An addiction cannot be managed alone. This requires the support and cooperation of a network of supporters. I was determined to provide this support to Henry.

They reel to and fro, and stagger
like a drunken man, and are at
their wit's end. Then they
cry unto the LORD in their

trouble, and He bringeth them out of their distresses.
Psalm 107:27-28

Henry frequently agreed to quit. During these times, we would lock up in our home. The kids were left with my mother. They didn't need to see what was happening. We would try to secure medication to help with the withdrawal symptoms.

Withdrawal for the average addicts may occur as early as a few hours after the last administration. With the passage of time, it increases in intensity before peaking. This produces drug cravings, restlessness, muscle and bone pain, insomnia, diarrhea and vomiting, cold flashes with goose bumps (cold turkey), kicking movements (kicking the habit), and other symptoms. Major withdrawal symptoms peak between 48 and 72 hours after the last dose and subside after about a week. Sudden withdrawal by heavily dependent addicts who are in poor health is occasionally fatal. However, heroin withdrawal is considered much less dangerous than alcohol withdrawal. I have seen both.

For their vine is of the vine of Sodom, and of the fields of Gomorrah: their grapes are grapes of gall, their clusters are bitter: Their wine is the poison of dragons, and the cruel venom of asps.
Deuteronomy 32:32-33

During the times I was incarcerated at the county jail, there were alcoholics who were confined there. If they were confined too long, this was prone to be an interesting time. While the alcoholics were normally boisterous or profane during intoxication, other outward displays of their addiction occurred as the drug wore off. Yes, alcohol is a drug. Severe alcohol withdrawals are often accompanied by hallucinations. Occasionally, the hallucinations were so extreme that everyone in the cell experienced difficulty resting or sleeping.

Once there was an elderly lady in our cell. She was going through severe alcohol withdrawals. Frequently, she jumped into the shower fully clothed. At other times, she stood around the cell making strange sounds. She constantly talked about hearing a baby crying. People in the cell talked about her. During the night, she walked around the cell, standing outside of our doors. Eventually, she was transferred to the mental hospital for treatment.

During the times when Henry was purposely withdrawing, he drank large amounts of juices and took multiple vitamins. During heroin detox, the body needs extra large quantities of nutrients to help the addict go through the effects of heroin withdrawal. We stayed in bed during most of the withdrawal cycle. I held him close to me, often massaging him. During these times, Henry was often unwilling or unable to talk on the telephone. He didn't want his family to see him in this condition. For this, I was ridiculed and drew the brunt of their criticism. As they had no idea what was going on inside the home, they assumed I was keeping him away from them. It was during these times that some people began to think that he was "hen-pecked."

But now listen to this, you afflicted ones, who sit in a drunken stupor, though not from drinking wine.
Isaiah 51:21 NLT

The physical and mental reactions to no longer taking drugs can be ghastly. The addict may go into convulsions. I never saw this happen to Henry. These convulsions can be so severe and frightening that the addict becomes afraid of them and returns to the drugs. If no medications are given during withdrawal, withdrawing from heroin is usually a three to five day period of discomfort. When it was possible, Henry took something to ease the symptoms.

Heroin affects many parts of the human body, including blood vessels that lead to the lungs, liver, kidneys and brain. It's been years since Henry stopped using heroin and began using crack. However, heroin left its mark. There are still occasions when he will begin to kick in his sleep. Assuming he was having a nightmare, I would often wake him.

The short-term effects of using heroin are:

- "Rush" or "High"
- Depressed respiration
- Clouded mental functioning

- Nausea and vomiting
- Spontaneous abortion
- Suppression of pain

The long-term effects of heroin are:

- Addiction
- Infectious diseases, for example, HIV/AIDS and hepatitis B and C
- Collapsed veins
- Bacterial infections
- Abscesses
- Infection of heart lining and valves
- Arthritis and other rheumatoid problems

The effects of cocaine also include increased heart rate, higher blood pressure, and accelerated breathing rates. Anxiety, restlessness, inability to sleep and loss of appetite leading to weight loss are characteristic with cocaine usage. Cold sweats, convulsions, vomiting and nausea may also occur.

Know ye not that the unrighteous shall not inherit the kingdom of God? Be not deceived: neither fornicators, nor idolaters, nor adulterers, nor effeminate, nor abusers of themselves with mankind, nor thieves, nor covetous, nor drunkards, nor revilers, nor extortioners, shall inherit the kingdom of God.

1 Corinthians 6:9-10

Drug usage can interfere with judgment about risk-taking behavior, and can potentially lead to reduced precautions about having sex, the sharing of needles, and the trading of sex for drugs, by both men and women. This includes prohibitions about having sex with same sex partners. Henry insisted that he has never shared his works (needles). This was something that I needed to believe. However, I seriously doubt the truth of his words. We know a number of people who have been infected with HIV/AIDS. Recently, I was tested again. By the grace of God, my results were negative.

The more serious effects of cocaine are heart attack, stroke and convulsions. A major effect of cocaine use is that cocaine addicts often continue using cocaine despite the above negative effects. The cocaine addict is chasing after the perfect high and will tolerate a lot of negative cocaine effects for a short-lived high. The effects of cocaine are instantaneous, extremely enjoyable, and temporary. Cocaine use creates high blood pressure and can cause heart attacks in even healthy individuals.

Crack is a different monster than heroin or cocaine. This drug brings on a new set of issues. If at all possible, crack took a deeper and lasting hold on Henry. Cocaine and crack both produce intense but short-lived elation and can make users feel more vigorous.

Crack is a version of powdered cocaine; however, crack is much more powerful. Crack is cooked into a more concentrated version of the normal powdered cocaine. Usually, crack is smoked through a glass pipe or aluminum can. Even though the possibility of death is just around the corner, the addict continues to abuse crack without concern.

Many former crack addicts have reported feeling "drugged" six months after they have stopped using drugs. Some addicts who quit using crack have reported feeling high on crack months after their last use. Months or years after they stopped using drugs, other former crack addicts report paranoia, anxiety, stress and many crack withdrawal feelings. Other addicts report that they still feel physical cravings for crack. Crack addiction has long-term effects on the brain and body of the addict.

Crack and other forms of cocaine can cause feelings of anxiety and depression, which may last for weeks. The depression may be severe enough to lead to suicidal thoughts or attempts. This overpowering addiction can cause the addict to do anything to get the drug. Anything means just that - ANYTHING! The destruction of property, personal health, and relationships with family, friends and co-workers are the side effects of crack addiction.

Grandchildren are the crowning
glory of the aged; parents are the
pride of their children.
Proverbs 17:6 NLT

Crack has directly contributed to the number of children in state foster care programs. This drug has also contributed to the number of elderly grandparents who are now raising a second or third generation of grandchildren. Even sadder, some children are forcibly raised without appropriate adult supervision. For many addicts, this appears a small price to pay for a temporary escape.

Recently, I spoke to a group of women at a substance abuse program. My daughter, Earline accompanied me to the program. In the course of the discussion, I was asked how my life style had affected my children. I encouraged my daughter to answer this question. Her memories of my past are very different from mine. Although I believe that my children were protected from my life style, Earline views this as neglect. What we remember and what our children remember about us are often very different. Youthfulness can hinder our perceptions. Drug usage may also cloud or distort reality.

Crack causes the abuser to feel a sense of worthlessness. This feeling of worthlessness is only one of the emotional effects of crack. The person becomes so emotionally beaten down by the use of this drug that they even lose interest in their own life. They begin to push people out of their lives until they are virtually in complete isolation. This isolation often results in chronic depression and furthers the addiction cycle.

Crack became very popular during the early eighties because of its highly addictive nature and easy accessibility on the streets. This was a cheap high. From the time crack hit the streets, it has claimed thousands of lives and continues to destroy thousands more each year. Stereotypically, crack has been seen as a 'homeless person's drug'. However, drug addiction does not discriminate. Drugs have destroyed many educated, promising, and economically advantaged individuals and families. Addiction does not discriminate and it does not care about the race, sex, class, or the age of the person it is destroying.

When crack hit the streets, it produced a new kind of criminal. They were willing to steal from their families and friends to support the high. Other addicts borrowed from family and friends to support the high. I often referred to it as the drug of petty criminals. When it emerged, it was not the drug of choice for career criminals. This has changed. Crack produced a more dangerous and desperate criminal.

Once a person is taken into the grips of crack, the person can no longer think clearly or rationally about life. Crack addicts can no longer make sound decision and lose sight of reality and anything that is important to their life.

The long-term effects of crack affect the user physically, mentally, and emotionally. These effects vary from person to person depending on the length and severity of the abuse. In general, the long-term effects of crack include restlessness, mood change, irritability, auditory hallucinations, and extreme paranoia.

During Henry's incarceration from 1987 through 1988, the drug gained popularity among his peers. Upon his release from prison, he began selling the drug. For a short time, he remained drug-free. Inevitably, he went back to intravenous heroin and cocaine usage. On March 26, 1989, he was arrested on multiple drug-related charges. This was less than five months after his release. He was still on parole.

Mama #2 made sure that he was released before a parole revocation prevented him from making bond. If his parole officer discovered his arrest, he could place a hold on him that would prevent him from being released from jail. Additionally if the parole officer decided that Henry had violated the terms of his parole, he could recommend that he be returned to prison to complete the remainder of his sentence. With Henry's record, this was almost a certainty.

After being released on bond, Henry left town. He eventually ended up hiding out in Atlanta. I went there frequently to visit him. He started slipping home to visit me and after a couple of months, we were back together. He was still abusing heroin. This threatened to destroy our relationship. However, in January of 1990, I renewed my relationship with Christ. This saved our marriage. Henry began going to church with me. He stayed clear of heroin usage for a while. He secured legal employment and for about a year remained drug-free.

Somehow, he got the notion that it would be easier to hide crack usage from me. There would be no new tracks. Tracks are scars caused by collapsed veins. After repeatedly injecting drugs into the same vein, the vein will collapse. Whenever, I was suspicious of his drug usage, I checked for fresh tracks.

In early 1991, I became aware that he was abusing some illegal drug. I wasn't sure what it was. Eventually, he admitted that he was using crack.

Crack is most often packaged in vials or plastic bags and sold in small quantities. As with any street drug, what is sold may not be what it is reported to be. Predicting side effects is difficult when the actual contents of the drug are not known.

Crack sometimes makes the user feel superior, in control, and psychic. These delusions are extreme and decrease when the drug wears off. Because crack can make the person feel high artificially without the usual demands that reality requires: success, being acknowledged, etc., crack seems like a shortcut to pleasure and success. The idea that crack improves life is the major LIE that crack users secretly hang onto. Their main objective is to get more crack. They lie very convincingly to friends and family. They lie to themselves.

After living in a state of denial or artificial success for an extended period of time, it can become difficult to separate a lie from reality. The denial that is associated with crack may continue after the addict has stopped using. Crack use leaves drug residues in the body; including the brain, liver and other tissues.

Crack denial is strong enough for the addict to believe they aren't addicted, even after spending time on the streets and in prison. Even having close encounters with death and seeing friends die as a result of using the drug does not shatter the denial. One of my friends had a heart attack as a result of his drug usage. He spent a number of years in prison. In spite of these consequences, he was reported to have returned to his drug usage. Crack denial is so strong that even death no longer scares the drug addict. In order for the addict to effectively recover, crack denial must first be broken. Denial must be broken in order for the addict to find a new way of life away from the bondage of drugs.

Although the crack denial of the addict is often the strongest, the people around them may also suffer from some form of denial. They don't want to feel the pain associated with the addiction. Family members and close friends stay in denial about the drug addiction of a loved one because they fear what will happen if they admit the truth. This denial is used as a defense mechanism. This type of avoidance usually causes more damage than good, and lets the addict continue in self-destructive behavior.

For all this I considered in my
heart even to declare all this, that
the righteous, and the wise, and
their works, are in the hand of God:
no man knoweth either love or
hatred by all that is before them.
Ecclesiastes 9:1

An addict uses drugs as a solution to their problems. Not dealing with problems often causes more problems. To completely end drug addiction a person has to feel more competent and develop better coping skills for living without drug usage.

Conquering an addiction requires more than abstaining from the addictive behavior or activity. This involves examining and changing all the associated feelings and behaviors attached to the addiction. The denial associated with the drugs often hinders this from happening. The formidable task of altering the addict's behavior and ultimately helping them in overcoming their addiction is made doubly hard because, in order for this to happen, the behavior of the codependent also needs to change.

Jesus said to him, "Go your way. Your
faith has healed you." And instantly

the blind man could see! Then he followed Jesus down the road.
Mark 10:52 NLT

When I changed my behavior towards Henry, it changed our relationship. His Mama #2 decided to show tough love. Henry didn't like tough love. While I firmly stood my ground, he resisted making these changes. His rebellion turned to hurt and pain. I couldn't see the pain. I hadn't turned against him. However, I had come to realize that I had contributed to the problems that he was having. It was difficult for him to relate to a Charlotte who wasn't catering to his every need. I was trying to teach him a different lesson. In order for him to become the head of the household, he needed to take responsibility for his actions and behavior.

For years, I had been Mama #2. Whenever he stumbled, I had been there to catch him. No matter what he did, I had tried to correct the problem. In many ways, I was enabling the very behavior that I hated. When I began catering to his needs, this was not my intention. I didn't want Henry to face the full consequences of his actions. Inadvertently, I was hindering his recovery. These consequences needed to be faced if the actions were going to cease.

Physical Effects of Crack

- chronic sore throat
- hoarseness
- shortness of breath
- bronchitis

- lung cancer
- emphysema and other lung damage
- respiratory problems such as congestion of
- the lungs, wheezing, and spitting up black phlegm
- burning of the lips, tongue, and throat
- slowed digestion
- weight loss
- high incidence of dependence
- blood vessel constriction
- increased blood pressure
- increased heart rate
- brain seizures that can result in suffocation
- dilated pupils
- sweating
- rise in blood sugar levels and body
- temperature
- disability from drug-induced health problems
- suppressed desire for food, sex, friends,
- family, and social contacts
- heart attack
- stroke
- death

Crack denial can be extreme. Crack denial is the belief that a problem doesn't exist. Crack denial is so powerful because crack is such an extreme drug that it is able to distort reality in the mind of the user. This denial or mindset can become a way of life. Denial may continue years after an addict discontinues drug usage. In order for an addict to fully recover, crack denial must be overcome. This is something I have only recently come to understand.

Perhaps, this knowledge came too late.

When Henry returned home in October of 2003, it was obvious that something was wrong with him. There was an almost immediate concern for his health. Yet, I didn't associate the symptoms with long-term drug usage. Rather, I assumed that something traumatic had occurred during his last incarceration. I also considered the possibility of a mild stroke or early dementia. For a number of years, the only obvious signs of his drug usage had been the tracks that scared his body. In the absence of drug usage, these got better.

The denial made it impossible for us to pick up where we left off. That place didn't exist anymore. Henry had his own ideas. He saw nothing wrong with himself. Not only was he defensive, sometimes, he took the offensive. This was to draw attention away from him. After a few weeks, it was obvious there was something seriously wrong. I questioned Henry but he denied that anything had happened during his last incarceration.

Although I was familiar with many short-term effects of drug usage and many of the obvious long-term effects of drug usage, I was confused by what was happening. I didn't know about the lingering effects of crack. Some of the outward physical effects were obvious, rapid aging, dental decay, and accelerated graying. My knowledge of heroin was more thorough.

Behold, Thou hast instructed many,
and Thou hast strengthened the
weak hands. Thy words have

upholden him that was falling,
and Thou hast strengthened
the feeble knees.
Job 4:3-4

Over the years, I had supported Henry through numerous difficult situations. Even in this situation, I was willing to help him. As I considered the physical effects of the drugs, I never considered the emotional or psychological effects of the drugs. Perhaps, this is the cruelest effect of the drugs.

Somehow, I had been lulled into a false sense of security. This may have been my own form of denial to cope with his drug usage. I needed to believe that once he stopped using drugs, we would have a normal life. My major concern had been with his overdosing. Sure, I had seen the commercials, read the books, and watched the films. It never became real.

Henry's reflexes were obviously slowed. There were also dental problems. He was having problems with critical thinking. Earline and I were concerned. Actually, concern is a mild way of saying it. We knew several people who had died directly or indirectly from crack usage. Henry was defensive about his health and actions. As we questioned him about what had happened, he became increasingly defensive. He tried to prove we were imagining the signs.

I will therefore that men pray
everywhere, lifting up holy hands,

without wrath and doubting.
1 Timothy 2:8

It seemed that I was living with a stranger. In order for our relationship to survive, something would have to change. Henry had been abusing these drugs for many years. It was unrealistic to think he would be spared the long-term effects of the drugs. Over the years, he had used heroin, cocaine, crack, Ritalin, and marijuana. These were just some of the drugs that he had used.

In spite of these overwhelming facts, God had provided a wonderful solution to all of our problems. All of our frustrations and problems could be poured out to God in prayer. With the confident knowledge that our God was still in charge, His grace would allow us to face all the challenges of tomorrow. Each time I touched Henry, I prayed for God to restore his health. We began drinking water constantly. God blessed him and the physical problems began to decline. His reflexes also improved.

A Messenger's Example

Who can say but that you have been elevated to the palace for just such a time as this?
Esther 4:14 NLT

For years, I have been drawn to the prophet Hosea. In fact, the ministry that God has given me is very close to the one he gave this prophet. As Hosea lived his message, I live the messages that God gives me.

Three years ago, a man walked up to me during a book signing. This was at a mall in Atlanta, GA. He asked me why the introduction to each of my books was written on page thirteen. He then told me that this was significant to the number of books that I would write. He said that there would be thirteen books. Actually, I probably have that many titles. However, when he gave me this information, I was not excited. Rather, I wondered what was going to happen in my life. My life has already taken so many crooks and turns.

My experiences are often relevant to the people that I meet who are in crisis. Recently, a young woman pulled her car in front of me; she began to tell me that she and her husband were in the midst of a divorce. She was still in shock. Over the Christmas holidays, a young lady approached me.

A man was conversing with me. She began to tell me her husband had been unfaithful. The man began to talk about his wife. They were also having marital problems. The young lady tried to convince him that his wife was having an affair. She didn't know his wife but she was doing a good job convincing him of his wife's infidelity. People passing by could hear the conversation. My activities had to cease for more than thirty minutes, as I attempted to restore some sanity to the situation. If God had not helped me recently through a similar situation, I wouldn't have handled this situation calmly. Perhaps, I would have chosen to ignore them.

The Book of Hosea is unique in the way it demonstrates the love of God towards His people. The life of the prophet Hosea is a living illustration to inspire and teach us, as well as an example for us to follow.

Hosea, a prophet of God, was married to Gomer. There was something terribly broken within Gomer. Hosea's wife was often unfaithful to him. Actually, she fell so low as to become first a prostitute, then a slave on the auction block. Even though she had dishonored and forsaken him and the children, God told Hosea to love and redeem her in the same way God loves and redeems us. Gomer was drawn to worldly lovers. Her wanderings took her far from home and off into a world of sin, a life of desperation and amnesia. Her spiritual life faded from her and drifted far from her. Her true identity slipped away from her into a sea of forgetfulness out among the heathen nations.

The story of Hosea and his wayward wife,

Gomer, has been told and retold. It is one of the most extraordinary stories of redemption and unconditional love in all of literature. As Hosea responded to God's instruction to take a prostitute for a wife, he was preparing to act out the relationship between God and His covenant people. Did knowing that God had a plan and purpose for the pain and humiliation that he endured lessen his own pain? I think not.

Thankfully, this wasn't the end of the story. Her lovers eventually scorned Gomer. She fell onto hard times, being an outcast from the nations. She eventually came into great tribulation. Here is where we begin to pick up the redemptive elements woven into the story. Hosea ultimately found her being offered up for sale in a slave market. Hosea purchased her for fifteen pieces of silver, five bushels of barley and a measure of wine.

In the Valley of Achor, she remembered her true husband and came to love him. Ultimately, Gomer was restored to the God of Abraham, Isaac and Jacob as His bride. The life of Gomer was a tragedy but in the manner of a true love story, it had a happy ending. It is also a vivid corroboration of that great devastation which is divorce. Jesus showed the same compassion and unconditional love to fallen humanity when He refused to allow the self-righteous to stone the woman caught in adultery. His instruction to her was to stop sinning after forgiving her.

In my case, it wasn't an adulterous husband that I continuously reclaimed. It was a drug addict. While adultery has occurred more than once in our marriage, this has not been the primary problem. The drug addiction and the effects of the drugs have been the culprits. Adultery comes with the lifestyle. Because of the honesty revealed in my books, some have mistakenly assumed that I am critical of my husband. Actually, the criticism is of the drugs and damage caused by a drug-induced criminal lifestyle.

In Henry, I see untapped potential. When I look at him, I see what he has the potential to become. I see the person hidden within him. He has accomplished more than many people thought was possible. Since I met him, not only has the length of his sober times increased, he has spent longer periods of time free from prison. Henry is a warm and compassionate person. This is the way that Hosea looked at Gomer. He continuously looked beyond her faults to see her needs. He did this by God's direction. This is a picture of how God looks at us in our fallen state. He looks beyond our brokenness to see what we have the potential to become for His glory.

For this, Thou shalt not commit adultery, Thou shalt not kill, Thou shalt not steal, Thou shalt not bear false witness, Thou shalt not covet; and if there be any other commandment, it is briefly comprehended in this saying, namely, Thou shalt love thy

neighbour as thyself.
Romans 13:9

Some people believe that drug addiction only strikes weak people. On the contrary, people who believe they are strong are often tempted to try the drugs. Drugs will destroy a person with the strongest resolve. Drugs have destroyed many good people and many families. No child sets a goal to become a drug addict, a prostitute, a thief, an abuser, a rapist, or a molester.

Sin is a cruel taskmaster. Jesus hates sin but he loves the sinner. I love Henry but I hate what the drugs have done to his life. The children love him but they fear the devastation that drugs have caused.

There are many opinions as to what is an appropriate marriage. There are changing legal and cultural definitions that often distort the picture God gave us in the Bible. Since God Himself is the author of marriage, only His opinion matters.

Divorce should not impede our continued attempts at a godly reconciliation, until one spouse remarries or refuses reconciliation in such a way as to reveal themselves to be, in effect, an unbeliever. Attempts to reconcile are an imperative after an un-Biblical divorce. Reconciliation should also be encouraged in the case of Biblical divorce, that God may be glorified in the restoration of relationships among his people.

We should remember the story of Hosea and Gomer. Within her, there was something painfully broken. This caused her to look for satisfaction and happiness in worldly pleasures. We should forever remember the story of a love that reached beyond the breaks. We should be reminded to hear what the person isn't saying, that we too might reach beyond the break to restore fallen humanity. When we reach below the surface to find the source of the hurt, we will find the source of the break. The hurt can be plucked up from the root. Once plucked up from the root, the source of the hurt/break can be destroyed. Once this happens, the cord can be mended together again. The person can then move on, and thus become a productive life for Christ.

The person, who has been forgiven much, will love much, and have a greater testimony for Christ. With the commitment and determination of Hosea, we should help each other reach beyond the breaks in our lives. However, before we can restore others, we must reach beyond the breaks in our own lives. This is often a painful process.

A break is anything that seeks to keep you trapped in a place of complacency, destroying the purpose and plan of God for our life. Sometimes, I refer to it as "Stuck on Stupid." In my own life, one break led to other breaks that almost destroyed me. If it hadn't been for the Lord on my side, surely I would have been consumed by the multitude of my transgressions.

Varetta

A.K.A. LORETTA DIANE JOHNSON
A.K.A. VORETTA DIANE JOHNSON
A.K.A. WARETTA DIANE JOHNSON
A.K.A. DEBRA JONES
A.K.A.VARETTA WILLIAMS
A.K.A VARETTA DIANE WILLIAMS

This chapter discusses my husband's ex-wife and how their marriage ended. She was a minor character in the other books but needs to be reintroduced in this book. Current circumstances have made this unavoidable. In an effort to be fair and unbiased, I will paraphrase a portion of Henry's version of my previous book, *The Flip Side*. In the previous book, I changed her name to Valerie. However, some information is a matter of public record. There is no longer a reason to conceal her true identity.

"Have I lied to anyone
or deceived anyone?
Job 31:5 NLT

In 1979, Henry was incarcerated at a county camp in Columbus, Georgia. It was here that he met a young lady from Atlanta. He met her through a guy who was serving time at the same camp. Henry describes her as nice looking, and a sharp dresser, who had a decent personality. She also had a good job. His friend provided him with this information before he met her. In prison, it is very common for inmates to introduce each other to people on the outside. These people are often exploited for the inmates' needs. While in prison, it is important to receive money, letters, visits, and gift packages from the outside. This provides the inmate with emotional support and serves as a status symbol. Varetta started coming to visit him at the prison. After getting acquainted with her, Henry thought this might be someone with whom he could spend his life.

Soon all you captives will be
released! Imprisonment, starvation,
and death will not be your fate!
Isaiah 51:14 NLT

Previously, Henry had served time at this camp. He had also escaped from the camp (Columbus Correctional Institute) before. Freedom started lingering on his mind. It seemed a good idea to put some of his time on an installment plan. Henry decided he was not going to complete his sentence at that time. He decided to release himself from the penal system and to return only if he was caught. His decision to leave was not influenced by his relationship with Varetta.

His work detail involved working in the shop

next to the prison. For about three months, Henry saved his money. He sent word for a friend to pick him up near the prison. The garbage trucks provided easy access for a ride away from the prison. After checking the route for each truck, Henry decided which one he would use for his escape. The hopper of the truck would make a perfect hiding place. The inmates working the back of the truck wouldn't give him away. Henry waited for a week for his friend to get back with him. After Henry didn't hear from him, he had to adjust his plan. He asked Varetta to pick him up at the shop. She drove down the side street and turned around. When she returned, Henry jumped in the back seat and lay down. It went off without a hitch.

After making sure they hadn't been followed, she took him to a friend's house. His friend was expecting him. His friend called another friend to come get him. He picked him up from her house and hid him until about nine that night. He drove him to Atlanta to a mall. Another friend picked him up from the mall.

The next day, Henry bought additional clothing and a plane ticket to New York. He knew where to find his homeboys. The cab dropped him off on the block (the place where his friends from Columbus hung out). In twenty minutes, Henry found one of his friends. They hooked up with two more friends from Columbus.

At this time, the heroin trade was on the decline in New York. There was a new trend emerging. People were freebasing cocaine. They decided to take their heroin and hit the road. They went to

Connecticut and opened shop. That state was still an open market for the heroin trade. Connecticut was close enough for them to have some knowledge of the drug culture there. They worked the area for about five months.

They will be rounded up and put
in prison until they are
tried and condemned.
Isaiah 24:22 NLT

When they left Connecticut, they went to Washington D. C. After being there for about a week, they went on to Atlanta. They worked Atlanta for three or four months. Inevitably, Henry caught another case that sent him back to finish the time he had left on installment. Henry completed his sentence at another prison, far from home.

In early 1983, Henry was released from prison on parole. Henry reported to the parole office only a couple of times. Almost immediately, Henry started medicating again. After seven months on parole, He was locked up again. There were four months left on the sentence. The parole revocation resulted in his serving the remainder of this time.

After his release in December 1983, Henry went to Abbeville, Alabama to live for a while. Varetta went with him. They stayed with his relatives. They had kept in contact throughout the years. She had also visited him several times in New York. They stayed in Abbeville for almost four months. Varetta and Henry were separated before he was locked up. During this time, they were trying to reconcile but they were still having problems. Inevitably, she went back to Atlanta. One day, she called him and Henry took a bus to Atlanta.

His uncle lived in Atlanta. He agreed to let Henry stay with him. His uncle had a business manufacturing security doors and windows. He was willing to provide him with a temporary job. After a short period, Henry was able to secure a job with a local construction company. This provided an avenue for him to get on his feet. After a couple of weeks, Henry moved into a boarding house.

Henry's relationship with Varetta was deteriorating. She was caught up in her own activities and habits. He was unhappy. Things weren't going right for him. The desire to medicate his problems began to tug at him. When Henry met me, he had been in his own private hell for years. He was looking for a change. In fact, he was praying for a change. His prayer was very specific, "God send someone into my life who has beauty on the inside."

His problems were closing in around him. He decided to come to Columbus for the weekend. It was during this trip that he met me. It had been several months since he had been involved with any woman. We spent the weekend together, and scheduled a date for the following weekend.

Henry failed to make our date for that Friday night. Since he didn't have a telephone, the next morning I drove to Atlanta to see him. There were so many problems with the boarding house; he was ready to move. Upon my arrival, he began packing his clothes. As Henry packed, we talked about our previous weekend. We talked about what had been good. We also talked about things that could be better.

After we took care of the loose ends in Atlanta, we headed to Columbus. We never really discussed the next step in our relationship. When we arrived, we went to my apartment. We unpacked the car as if it was understood; Henry was moving in with me. He was originally supposed to be visiting me for a week.

Things were moving fast between us. Whatever his original thoughts were about our relationship, they were changing quickly. I did more than smile at him. In the beginning, I catered to him. There was another side of me that Henry didn't know. My showing up on his doorstep should have been an indication but he didn't catch the hint. I am a very determined, willful, and strong spirited woman. Additionally, I am full of surprises. It was hard for him to be bored around me. I kept him entertained and laughing. As the relationship progressed, Henry would learn I had a lot of nerve.

Henry called his mother to let her know he was in town. He also informed her that he would be bringing guest home for Sunday dinner. In celebration of Mother's Day, his sister was barbecuing and everybody was bringing a covered dish. Henry didn't eat pork. When we arrived at his sister's house with the children, we brought chicken, steaks, and beef ribs. His mother lived next door to his sister.

One of his sisters commented about how long Henry had been involved with me. She was sure it had been going on for an extended period. Henry thought she had heard something on the street. He told her it had only been a week. She thought he was lying. It was hard to hide the comfort we felt with each other. Henry was comfortable with the children, too. They were comfortable with him.

At the end of the week, Henry was enjoying our new relationship. I told him that he could stay in Columbus. This was appealing to him. We went back to Atlanta to pick up the rest of his belongings. Henry was moving in with me. This wouldn't be a one-night stand or a weekend fling.

It wasn't long before his addiction flared up full force. Each day, Henry would use my car to go stealing with his friends. He would leave me waiting for his return. After he scored, he would pick me up to help him sell the merchandise. One day, Henry went to take off a lick (steal something from a location he had scouted out previously). I was waiting for him on Ninth Street. The guys with him were scared to go through with it. However, Henry was determined to complete the mission. He knew someone who had the heart to help him.

"Man, let me go get my woman," Henry said.

They came back to Ninth Street and Henry told me what he had in mind. Just as he thought, I was game to help him pull it off. This went off without a hitch. This changed the way we did business. From then on, I was going with him. If it was a heavy job, I was the driver to aid our escape. If it was clothing, I picked and organized the outfits.

I loved clothes. I was sure my needs were

considered in every bag that they took. Sometimes, his partners got upset because I wanted so many outfits. In the end, I got every outfit that I wanted. I also had to have shoes and stockings to match each outfit. Henry nicknamed me 'Sporty O'tee.' I wore a new outfit every day. Dressing in this fashion made it easy to steal. I looked rich. It was also easy for me to converse with store employees.

Money was rolling into the house. This gave us a double cut on the ventures involving other people. Drugs consumed most of his money. I smoked reefer and drank expensive champagne. Nevertheless, I made sure everything at the house was covered. One day of each month was used to supply the house with food, toiletries, and clothes for the kids. We also stole the other necessities. We took one day a month to earn the money to pay the household bills. We hired babysitters to watch the kids. At night, we planned for the next day.

His relatives couldn't understand what was going on between us. Some of them tried to get him back with Varetta. We were caught up in the criminal lifestyle. The drugs put any remorse on hold.

We began to make bigger plans for stealing. Sometimes, it seemed we were running out of places to hit. His habit was getting worse. It was requiring greater quantities of drugs to prevent him from becoming sick. We often had to make a quick run to get the monkey (withdrawals) off his back. A small lick in the mornings would give him enough money to cop (purchase) enough drugs to ease his sickness. Once the initial sickness was over, we could hit the highway.

One day, as we were doing one of these quick hits, things went wrong. We did only limited stealing in Columbus. We seldom went downtown to steal. With the exception of a few stores, the kind of merchandise we were moving wasn't readily available there.

No one who trusts in you will ever be disgraced but disgrace comes to those who try to deceive others.
Psalms 25:3 NLT

We had hit some of the quick-fix spots too regularly. Henry needed his medication before we could travel. One day in desperation, we hit several stores downtown. Before long, we were stopped. We saw the policeman coming and we were able to hide the merchandise we were carrying. Since we didn't have anything on us, we didn't expect anything to come out of it. One of the store owners made a positive identification. We were taken to the jail. No merchandise had been found. The first day, it seemed as if they questioned us for hours.

At the end of the day, they found my car parked downtown. It was packed with excess merchandise we had been unable to sell. The name of the stores had been removed from most of the merchandise. With his record, Henry would have to enter a plea bargain.

After several days, we were allowed to make bond. They had prevented us from making bond to allow them time to identify the merchandise. Henry's addiction had worn off. When we were released, we went back to work. We needed money to pay a lawyer and the bondsman. There was one stipulation; we didn't mess with Columbus. We put the show on the road. The addiction was soon back.

After the night Ms. Doll asked Henry to call Varetta, we didn't hear from Varetta again until several weeks later. To complicate matters, things became strained between Henry and me when Varetta came to town. The visit came a little too late. Some members of his family were pressuring him to reconcile with her. Ms. Doll brought Varetta to our apartment. Varetta remained in the car. Ms. Doll came to the door of the apartment to tell him that Varetta needed to see him. When he walked to the car, they provided the excuse for their visit; the baby needed diapers. This child was not mentioned in *The Flip Side*, as it was assumed any doubts about his paternity had been settled.

Henry didn't have any children. He wanted desperately to believe the child was his son. He said the mother had engaged in other relationships, which led to their breakup. The night that I met him, he shared this with me.

"She was involved with other people. Financially, some of them were good to her. She wanted me to understand that it was just about the money. I couldn't accept this as part of our relationship."

Except for a few items provided for the child during the early years of his life, no financial or emotional support was provided for the child. Soon after the child's birth, Henry was told that someone else acknowledged the child and was providing financial support. This child is now a man. During the last twenty years, we had virtually no contact with the child or his mother. During the last fifteen years, he never mentioned either of them to me.

When Varetta arrived in town in August of 1984, Henry and I had been involved for several months. I had assumed several roles in his life. Not only was I operating in the role of his wife, I was also lover, crime partner, co-defendant, friend, and his constant companion. More than those relationships, another primary relationship was developing. I was becoming his second mother. It wasn't just that I washed his dirty clothes and cooked for him. The addiction and my co-dependency were driving our relationship.

The long-term result of living with an addict is a condition called co-dependency. This condition often leads to feelings of chronic anger and resentment, affects a person's ability to trust and feel intimate, and can lead to serious emotional problems.

When he was sick, I mopped up his vomit. Each day, as he went from one drug house to another, I sat in the car waiting for his return. Even as we continued this ritual, I made sure that he had a balanced diet. When drugs weren't causing interference, he had a hefty appetite. He could eat ten to fifteen chicken wings at once. Usually, I packed him a lunch when he left home in the morning. His friends teased him about the size of the lunches. During the day, we would purchase prepared food. Henry would eat fifteen Krystal hamburgers with ease. We often bought fried chicken. This didn't eliminate his desire for me to fry chicken when we returned home. He often ate from two plates, one for meat and bread, and another for vegetables. For added nutrients, he took daily vitamins.

At the end of each day, we returned home. As he continued to get high, I watched closely to make sure there were no signs that he was overdosing. Often, after I was asleep, he went out for more drugs. There were other times that he was unable to eat until two or three o'clock in the early morning. Whenever this happened, I cooked for him. Usually, I fried chicken wings for him.

It was a little late for me to quietly walk away. I had invested too much into the relationship. There was also the pending court date. When Ms. Doll told Henry that Varetta was waiting in the car for him, I walked to the car with him. His relatives couldn't understand what was going on between us. Since we had these cases, I wasn't going away. Henry felt pulled in several directions. The decision was taken out of his hands when he was locked back up.

Varetta came to see him at the jail. They talked about reconciling. They talked about what had gone wrong with their relationship. She was staying at his mother's house. He didn't want to make anybody angry. Rather than officially ending the relationship, he left it up in the air. His future was uncertain. He was involved in a relationship and a case with someone else. There were no guarantees as to how this would end. Additionally if he was locked up for an extended period, who was going to stand by him? He didn't want to get locked in on either side.

The next day, I went to see him. Things were still somewhat distorted between us. We needed to resolve our differences. If we didn't, it would leave room for the detectives to take advantage of the situation. We talked about our relationship and the cases. We were careful not to say anything that would help the detectives. We also talked about his visitor. In the end, he assured me that his relationship with Varetta was over. We reconciled our differences. Varetta didn't come back to the jail.

Two months later, we were sentenced. We agreed to a plea bargain. This was the only way to guarantee my freedom. Henry got a six-year split sentence, four years to serve in prison and two years on probation. I got probation.

In the fall of 1984, Henry was sent to a correctional camp in Hardwick, Georgia. It was a state camp but it had county camp mentality. It was sweet in a lot of ways. This afforded him some opportunities, which often reminded him of being free. In the end, it was too sweet. He made some careless mistakes that brought heat on him. They also brought heat on me. I was selling marijuana on the streets. Henry was receiving regular money orders. Nevertheless, the temptation or greed was there. He wanted more money on the books. He also wanted to send money home. It seemed like a perfect plan. When he presented it to me, I was skeptical. It didn't take much for me to ignore the fear. The fear never went away; greed overrode it.

He was always greedy but never satisfied. Of all the things he dreamed about, nothing remains.
Job 20:20 NLT

Things went smoothly for a while. Henry got cocky. He wasn't satisfied moving the drugs inside the prison where he was incarcerated. He decided it would also be financially beneficial to move the drugs into the women's prison. Henry was attending classes there. He became involved with one of the women incarcerated there. He was providing drugs for her to sell at the women's prison. Their relationship was discovered. They were caught in a compromising position. This brought his activities at Rivers under scrutiny. This was hidden from me until sometime later.

The sweet prison turned sour. Henry was searched. No drugs were discovered. When I arrived at the prison, I was "strip searched." Henry tried to console me and reassure me but it didn't work. For months, I had been a regular visitor at the prison. I was familiar with many of the officers and the regular visitors at the prison. When I was singled out to be searched, it was humiliating. My privacy was invaded by the search. I hated the thought of taking my clothes off in front of a stranger. I felt like a prisoner. We had violated the rules of the prison but we never considered the weight of the consequences.

Within a week, I had him moved to another prison. This was better for both of us. He was closer to home. His time at Rutledge went smoothly. I was still working the drug business. We put a hold on his end of it. Henry enrolled in a program to enable him to become a licensed barber. In spite of this, he planned to return to crime when he was released.

It was less than a month before his release. When I went to see Henry, I told him that I had been arrested. He was shocked. This was not the way he had things planned. I also told him that I had given my life back to God. He was glad about this. However, this began a new cycle in our life.

So she cried whenever she was with him and kept it up for the rest of the celebration. At last, on the seventh day, he told her the answer because of her persistent nagging.
Judges 14:17a

He knew a lot of things about me. During this period, he found out something new, I was a nag. I wanted us to get married. I wanted him to stop doing drugs. Most of all, I wanted him to be “saved”. I harped on this every time I came to see him. Henry promised me that he would do right by me when he was released. The desire to medicate was still there. As his release date grew closer, the desire to medicate increased. It became stronger and more urgent.

It is better to dwell in a corner of
the housetop, than with a brawling
woman in a wide house.
Proverbs 21:9

The day he was released, I picked him up from the prison. He wanted to stop by Herb's house. I was uncomfortable with this stop. Henry kept his true intentions hidden from me. As I was sitting on the porch with Herb's wife, he took his medication in the bathroom. It didn't take long for me to figure it out. This was when the nagging escalated.

The next day, he reported to the parole office. His parole officer told him that we wouldn't be able to live together. Henry asked him why.

"She's your co-defendant," the parole officer said.

Henry assured him that was in the past. He told him that I had changed. He thought this was an excuse. He also insulted Henry by calling him, John Henry. This was a reference to *The Legend of John Henry.* The story of John Henry, told mostly through ballads and work songs, traveled from coast to coast as the railroads drove west during the 19th

Century. It has become timeless, spanning a century of generations with versions ranging from prisoners recorded at Mississippi's Parchman Farm in the late 1940s to present-day folk heroes. Like Paul Bunyan, John Henry's life was about power. It was about the individual, raw strength that no system could take from a man. It was also about weakness, the societal position in which he was thrust, being an ex-slave.

I don't know if the officer was comparing an ex-slave to an ex-convict or if it was more a reflection of Henry's size. John Henry was a big man. Henry was also tall. The officer was short in statue. At any rate, he understood that Henry was not amused by the name. He continued to use it.

When we left the parole office, we needed to come up with a plan. Stealing was his game. As a result of his parole officer's stipulations, he needed to steal time with me.

As it was growing closer to my court date, there was still no plea bargain. This was weighing heavily on Henry's mind. He didn't tell me. It was easier to keep his thoughts to himself. Medicating helped him pretend it wasn't going to happen; I wasn't going to prison. We talked constantly, when we were together. We tried to figure out a way to avoid my going to prison. He tried to convince me to leave town with him. I didn't want to spend the rest of my life running from the charges.

It would be easier if my co-defendant took the charges. With a previous drug conviction, things were stacked against her. That's when Henry decided to make her an offer. If she would cut me loose, he was willing to pay her. She would also have everything she needed before she went to court. She needed someone to look out for her.

As the court date drew closer, it looked worse. Finally, Henry decided that if I was going to prison, he was going to marry me before it happened. The salvation part could be put on hold.

My divorce from my first husband had been final for several months. However, there was a problem. Henry had filed for a divorce from Varetta but it wasn't final. Circumstances prevented him from being able to finalize his divorce before my court date. As usual, we figured out a plan for this. If it became apparent that I was going to be convicted, we would get married. He could take the final decree the next week.

We had taken the blood tests weeks earlier. He loved me but he wasn't ready to get married. The marriage was put off until the last minute. The possibility of my conviction was the primary reason for our marriage. If I wasn't convicted, we could delay the marriage. If I was convicted, there would be too many complications if we weren't married.

The day we had dreaded arrived. There were two sicknesses eating at him. His habit was calling but he had to be in court. His medication had to be worked around court. When the court recessed for lunch, we were married. For lunch we both had champagne. Henry also had some medication.

The laws of the state where the marriage took place determine the validity of a marriage. There are usually three possibilities concerning the legality of a marriage. Under Georgia law, my marriage to Henry would become legal when his divorce became final.

(1) The marriage was void, which means you need to get an annulment (or ruling of nullity, which amounts to the same thing) and then remarry;

(2) The marriage was voidable, which means unless someone has taken positive action to have it voided, it can be validated, either by legal action or by passage of time; or

(3) The marriage started out voidable but became valid automatically when your husband's divorce became final.

Where wife was married at time of ceremonial marriage to husband in Georgia in 1942 although she believed herself divorced at the time and wife obtained divorce from first husband in 1948 upon learning that she was not divorced and parties continued to live together in Georgia so as to consummate a valid common law marriage under the laws of that state, husband was not entitled to a divorce on grounds of prior subsisting marriage of wife at time of ceremonial marriage. Lightsey v. Lightsey, 56 Tenn. App. 394, 407 S.W.2d 684 (1966).

When I was locked up on September 2, 1986, the day after my first marriage to Henry, the plan was lost. As he was accustomed to dealing with any problem, he medicated. The medication required money that was acquired by stealing. He went on a stealing rampage and a binge.

The Lord said to me, "Go, show your love to your wife again, though she is loved by another and is an adulteress. Love her as the Lord loves the Israelites, though they turn to other gods..."
Hosea 3:1 NIV

Stealing with a female partner provides more flexibility. It draws less attention for the man to steal from the women's department if he's accompanied by a woman. Henry chose one of his previous partners. This was a sexual and business partner. The drug usage also limits sexual inhibitions. Yet it may hinder actual performance. Henry later told me this was the nature of their relationship. This wasn't a romantic liaison. They were friends; the other acts were a matter of drug-induced convenience. As I learned from Ms. Doll, the woman moved into our apartment. There were also a number of other people who were a part of the crew camping out there.

By the time Henry came to see me the first weekend, it was obvious that things were out of control. The effects of the binge were obvious. It could be seen in his hair, in his eyes, and the obvious weight loss. I warned him about what he was doing. He promised that he would gain control over his behavior. This was an empty promise. He was going down fast.

On September 20, 1986, eighteen days after I began my sentence, Henry was locked up. This happened faster than I had expected. He seemed relieved that it was over. He had only been out since May 14, 1986. He had barely been free four months. He was headed back to prison. With me being locked up, the chances of his making bond were almost obsolete. I don't think he even bothered to try.

He went through the withdrawals in jail. Because of an ability to communicate through the toilets at the jail, I supported him through the process.

On October 30, 1986, I was shipped to Hardwick, GA. This was where I completed my sentence. During that time, I learned many things about Henry's previous incarceration in the same city. He also had a history at the prison where I was confined. While incarcerated at Rivers Correctional Institute, Henry attended classes at the women's prison. He was involved with one of the inmates at the women's prison. The week after I arrived at the prison, she was brought back to the prison to serve another sentence. This information was quickly shared with me. This was an effort to break my spirit. I was vexed but I had bigger problems. The fifteen-year sentence that I was carrying was the biggest problem.

When I was released on August 1, 1987, Henry was confined at the state camp in Columbus, GA. One of the first things that needed to be corrected was his marital problem. The divorce needed to be finalized. I contacted a lawyer and Henry was mailed the papers in prison. On November 18, 1987, his divorce was final from Varetta.

Henry remained incarcerated until November 1, 1988. Varetta was also incarcerated from May

19, 1988, until February 23, 1989, for multiple theft charges. To my knowledge, they had no contact during their overlapping sentences. Later, they would have a second over lapping sentence. When Henry and I had overlapping sentences, he arranged to come visit me in prison.

Where's the Love?

"Husbands, love your wives, just as Christ also loved the church AND GAVE HIMSELF FOR HER"
Ephesians 5:25

The number one need of a man is companionship: having his wife as his playmate in things that interest him and give him relaxation and gratification. This is not the number one need of a woman. The number one need of a woman is affection. Due to their number one needs being different, it presents a problem. If a husband naturally expresses himself to his wife, he will overlook her needs to fulfill his own. If a wife naturally expresses herself to her husband, she will disregard his needs to accomplish her own.

He that is without a wife is
solicitous for the things that belong
to the Lord: how he may please God.
But he that is with a wife is
solicitous for the things of the
world: how he may please his wife.
And he is divided. And the
unmarried woman and the virgin

thinketh on the things of the Lord: that she may be holy both in body and in spirit. But she that is married thinketh on the things of the world: how she may please her husband.
1 Corinthians 7:32b-34

A major part of this lack of love in the family is because of the man's failure to derive from his wife the love that he needs. The husband has a vital role in producing the love, which is God's nature, in a family. A great responsibility is placed upon him by God to lay down his life for his family.

"Let the husband RENDER to his wife THE AFFECTION DUE her, and likewise, also the wife to her husband.... "
1 Corinthians 7:3-5

God's desire for the husband and wife is that they tenderly love (phileo) each other while they overlook each other's faults and failures (agape love). When the couple fails to express this type of love, it damages the marriage relationship. Because love often leaves us vulnerable to pain, we often desire to turn love off or discontinue loving. This is a great mystery. If only it were this simple: you have hurt me; therefore, I'm turning my love off. However, this is not the way that it works. Love is a matter of the heart, not the mind.

At some point in our relationship, Henry and I have both desired to end the love. There have been times that I have wanted to pray, "God kill whatever I feel for him." Wisdom has prevailed during those times. To end up trapped in a loveless marriage would bring greater difficulty. Love helps to heal the pain that relationships often bring.

Another kind of love needed in a marriage is storge. Storge is a tangible show of affection that results from a pure motive. Because males are different from females, the wife usually needs this kind of love more from her husband. It may be a hug, a kiss, or another expression of genuine affection. It is important for the husband to set aside his need of companionship and meet his wife's main need, which is affection.

Eros love is also required to fulfill a marriage relationship. Eros is the fulfillment of the physical sexual desire that a husband and wife express toward each other. It's when "...the two ...become one flesh" (Matthew 19:5). Love is supposed to be unconditional. Even in marriage, it's often hard to love this way. There is often a belief that we can change the person into what we want them to be.

Without knowing God, it's impossible to know, receive, or share real love. Without God, love is a selfish, self-seeking love. The expectations are often, "What can I gain from this relationship?"

Be ye not unequally yoked together
with unbelievers: for what
fellowship hath righteousness

with unrighteousness? and what communion hath light with darkness?
2 Corinthians 6:14

When these four types of love operate in a marriage, the marriage is complete. A picture of a complete marriage is a husband and wife who laid down their life for each other (agape love) no matter how many times the other offends them or causes them to have negative feelings. They both have tender inclinations toward each other (phileo love). They derive joy from each other's company because they're best friends. Because they delight in each other so much, they hug, kiss, hold hands and do pleasing things for their mate (storge love). Because their hearts are overflowing with agape, phileo and storge, a warm passionate desire arises within both of them to relish each other.

Defraud ye not one the other, except it be with consent for a time, that ye may give yourselves to fasting and prayer; and come together again, that Satan tempt you not for your incontinency.
1 Corinthians 7:5

There are some things that have always been good between Henry and me. Things were good when we put selfishness and pride aside. They were good when we followed God's instruction. The Bible gives specific instructions about fasting. In the past, I thought these instructions were provided to prevent lust from destroying a marriage. These instructions are provided for a much deeper reason. When spouses abstain from physical relationships or acts of affection, we allow a number of things to intervene in our relationships, rebellion, hurt, neglect, rejection, pride, and chaos.

Choose Ye

Since I know it is all for Christ's good, I am quite content with my weaknesses and with insults, hardships, persecutions, and calamities. For when I am weak, then I am strong.
2 Corinthians 12:10 NLT

God has a purpose and plan for marriage. While many desire a spouse or mate, there are various reasons for this desire. Some individuals hope to find completeness by uniting with another person. Some people marry for social, financial or material gain. Others marry for companionship or to avoid loneliness. Still, others marry to quench the fires burning in their flesh. This is not meant to be an exhaustive list of reasons for the commitment.

The Lord wants to save us from tragedy, sickness, fear, anxiety, and the turmoil of this world. These things come upon us because of our bad choices or through ignorance or chains of iniquity.

We face choices on a personal level daily. What will we eat? Who will we vote for? Whom will we marry? What occupation should we pursue? Should I return the money that was credited to my account accidentally? When only God is watching, what kind of choices do we make? He is looking for people He can trust as He desires to use us in His work. Should I purchase this item on credit? Do I really need this item or is it something I want, even though I cannot afford it?

Is the Word of God still true? Do we have a choice of which scriptures to obey? Are some sins greater than others are? Do we justify our sins by looking for fault in others? Does God give us instructions or directions that are contrary to his word? Are those who practice sinning at every opportunity members of the body of Christ? Is salvation a matter of convenience? At what point do we become a partaker in another man's sin? Has the Word of God become of non-effect? For all of the questions that I have posed, the answers are found in the Word of God. His word will never return void.

Abstain from all appearance of evil.
1 Thessalonians 5:22

These are just some samples of choices that we face. We also face temptations that we must resist with the Word of God. People addicted to drugs will go to great lengths to get drugs and continue to take them even when it hurts their relationships with their loved ones. This is a choice with long-term consequences.

The consequences of some choices are more deadly than others are. When we rebel against God and choose our own way, we are choosing a path that will ultimately end in destruction. Because of God's love and mercy to humanity, most of our choices do not have immediate results.

We are all given time to repent and find the Lord. We may get away with sinning for a while; however, in time, we will reap what we have sown.

The Lord is not slack concerning His promise, as some men count slackness; but is longsuffering to usward, not willing that any should perish but that all should come to repentance.
2 Peter 3:9

In every situation, we have choices. People or a system can imprison our physical bodies. However, we can choose to keep our minds free. Freedom comes from God. He gives us freedom that no one can take away.

"Don't store up treasures here on earth, where they can be eaten by moths and get rusty, and where thieves break in and steal. Store your treasures in heaven, where they will never become moth-eaten or rusty and where they will be safe from thieves. Wherever your treasure is, there your heart and thoughts will also be."
Matthew 6:19-21 NLT

We can't force someone to choose what God has allowed them the free will to reject. As soon as a person is born again, he should begin to make the choices that will put to death his old ways of thinking, talking, and acting, and allow the Holy Spirit to replace them with God's ways. God gave man the freedom of choice when He created Adam. God will not violate our free wills and make us do the right thing. He will not make choices for us. We can choose His way or reject it.

There are only two ways: God's way or the devil's way. What man thinks is his own way puts him under the authority of the enemy. If someone is not for God, he automatically is against Him. It is not possible that man can do his own thing and think he is not making a choice. Even "no choice" is a choice. When we refuse to choose, we allow others to make our choices for us. God wants us to make godly choices so that we may have His love, joy, peace, and victory over every trial and temptation that comes into our lives.

Our future is determined by all the choices we are making today. We have to allow God to help us make our decisions. This will determine whether our future will be secure and we will have God's blessing. As Joshua declared, "As for me and my house, we will serve the Lord." God promised Joshua good success if he obeyed the words of the Bible and chose to follow Him. Joshua and his family were blessed because he made the right choices. He was an overcomer! We can overcome the trials in our life when we make the right choices. Sometimes, it seems easier to make the wrong choice.

In recent months, I have been tempted to make several wrong choices. I have been tempted to follow ungodly advice. I have been tempted to do what seemed convenient. The old Charlotte has been waiting to rise up. Making the right decisions has been heart wrenching. Ultimately, I know that God is pleased with the choices that I have made. The most important choice that I have made was the choice to let Him straighten out every crisis in my life.

Trust Me

We who have fled to Him for refuge can take new courage, for we can hold on to His promise with confidence.
Hebrews 6:18-19

Trust is an essential ingredient for a healthy marriage, for intimacy, communication and love to grow. You can't have a healthy relationship without trust. The institution of marriage was created to provide the most fulfilling, satisfying, and mutually beneficial human relationship that we would ever experience. Trust begins and ends with God. Trusting another person has to have a certain expectation of failure and thus be combined with a willingness to forgive. People are human, frail, and sinful. Therefore, we need to have a realistic type of trust when we choose to trust people.

When Henry and I were married the first time, I made the decision to trust him. Although I was aware of his shortcomings, particularly the addiction, I wanted a **normal marriage**. Normal wasn't an option considering the circumstances. I was headed to prison. From the beginning of the relationship, I had handled the finances for the household. No matter how much money we made each day, whatever he didn't give me ultimately ended up in the hands of a drug dealer. With this knowledge, I took a terrible risk. In leaving Henry in control of the apartment, I stood to lose everything that I owned. After considering all the facts, I decided that I would take the risk. It wasn't the first time that I had opted to leave everything behind. I had always survived.

After I was sentenced, my family went to the apartment to pack my belongings. This was without my knowledge. When I discovered what had happened, I was angry. I explained that he was my husband and I was going to trust him. They didn't understand how I could take such a risk. Nevertheless, they agreed to abide by my decision. The apartment was returned to its original order.

Ms. Doll was the first person to tell me that Henry had violated my trust. When Henry was arrested a short time later, my family had to return to the apartment. This was when I got the second report. My mother was sure that some of my clothes were missing. Henry wouldn't admit to either one of the reports. He said that if any things were missing, he would make it up to me. Upon his release from prison, he kept his word.

Trusting grows in a relationship over time. During my incarceration, I learned to trust Henry for emotional support. However, I doubted his ability to be faithful and responsible. As you spend time together with someone, you build understanding and an expectation authenticity. You gain insight into the person's needs, motivations, and fears.

Unconditional love develops trust. When I was released from prison, I discovered that indeed some of my clothes were missing. It wasn't as many as I was expecting. Actually, I had so many clothes that it was hard to be sure what had disappeared. This was something that I should have expected. After all, Henry sold his own belongings.

Although this was the first time that he had taken something from me, I knew that Henry often pawned his own belongings. There was pair of alligator shoes that he pawned several times. During the night as I slept, this was done. When I discovered the shoes were missing, I would redeem them. He was also prone to pawn his jewelry.

This behavior was embarrassing to me. Rather than allowing someone to gloat at what his addiction was doing to him, I preferred to pay what he owed. Eventually, this reached a point where I said, forget it! Whenever I was asleep if he wasn't ready to stop getting high, he found something else to pawn.

We are a fallen people living in a fallen world. Put two of us together in a marital relationship and there will be failures. The trust will be violated, feelings will be hurt, and evil will be done. Faith comes from God. Our faith should be in God. God is the only One who is truly faithful. He is the giver of faith and the object of faith. Because of those facts, we need a new understanding of what it means to trust people.

We have to adjust our expectations. People are human, frail, and sinful. Therefore, we need a realistic type of trust when we choose to trust someone. We can trust God totally.

When Henry was released from prison in November of 1988, he began selling drugs. He kept his word to replace my clothes. He asked shoplifters to bring me clothes. If I wanted it, I bought it with his money. We put in orders for additional clothes. Each Sunday, he took me shopping. The first time we went shopping, I was shocked by the amount of money that he spent on one outfit. After that point, I came to expect this.

Over the years, the trust began to return. The only time that I didn't trust him was when drugs were involved. Under the influence of a mind-altering substance, no one can be trusted.

After the initial trust was broken, I never made the mistake of trusting the welfare of our home to Henry. For years, we have had a joint savings account. He has never been provided this information. Because of Henry's addiction and numerous incarcerations, most of the property was purchased in my name. These were matters that I never discussed with him. Whenever he asked about these areas, I had a smart retort ready.

Before our second marriage, I decided to trust him again. At least, I was planning to try. During this time, I was listening to a lot of teaching about unity in marriage. I wanted to try the **normal way** again. With time, I planned to share everything with him. This was the type of relationship that I wanted. Past experiences said that I should tread softly and carefully.

For many people trusting others is difficult. Some have been hurt by past relationships. Others have barriers that keep them from being able to trust. A couple needs to be aware of the obstacles to building trust. Building trust is a process. This involves taking a risk; if our partner responds in a favorable way, we are encouraged to risk again. Step by step, barriers are broken down and trust begins to take their place. This may take time but it must happen for a healthy relationship to be built.

Trust had been broken in our relationship. The trust needed to be restored. Although I had made several major decisions concerning my marriage to Henry, I kept them from him. He would have to show me that he was indeed trustworthy. There were many people who were aware that I had decided to change our relationship. When I asked Henry to work with me, it should have given him an indication. It didn't. At the time, I was convinced we could achieve almost anything if we applied the same diligence to doing right that we had applied to doing wrong.

But godliness with contentment
is great gain.
1 Timothy 6:6

When Henry decided that his goals were different than mine, I was terribly disappointed. He was still looking for immediate gratification; I was looking towards our future. Rather than working together as one, we were working to achieve something totally different. In many ways, rather than working with me, he was competing against me. There was absolutely no reason for this.

Our marriage became strained under the competition. When our house caught fire in June of 2004, things grew worse. When my credit cards disappeared temporarily, that incident was the breaking point. It wasn't just the credit cards. This meant I couldn't trust him. The risk I had taken was unwise. Within him was still the potential to destroy everything that I was working towards. Henry was adamant that he didn't take my credit cards. By the time he shared this with me, the second divorce was already final.

After we were remarried for the third time, trust needed to be reestablished. During our separation, Henry had been searching for a car. His dream car became the 2005 Chrysler 300. He shared this information with me and asked for my help. I wasn't familiar with the car. He had saved some money for a down payment. Henry said that his credit check was decent. I doubted that his credit was sufficient but agreed to accompany him to the car lot.

There was only one of the cars on the lot. It happened to be one my favorite colors. Henry wanted me to drive the car. It was an American-made car and I prefer foreign cars. For Henry sake, I tried to show interest in the car. Later, we drove to a second car lot several miles away. They didn't have any on the lot but were willing to try to locate one. When they pulled Henry's credit, I held my breath. The salesman returned to confirm my fears.

Looking at Henry, he said, "There is no way that we can put you in this car. How is your wife's credit?"

I didn't say a word. Henry was insistent. He had his heart set on that car.

He pleaded, "CJ please let him pull it. I'll do

whatever it takes to pay the note."

This was not setting well with me. We had another car less than a year old. This wasn't in the budget. I don't make rash financial decisions. Most of all, there was a nudge in my spirit that said, "NO!"

The salesman insisted that he just wanted to check my credit; I was under no obligations. Finally, I relented and allowed him to pull my credit report. He was gone for more than thirty minutes. I knew he was doing more than checking my credit; he was checking for financing. Henry continued his efforts to persuade me to get the car. In the end, it wasn't my conversation with Henry that swung my decision.

A few weeks earlier, I had a conversation with my brother-in-law. During our relationship, nothing had ever been in Henry's name. This was more of a security issue for me than a desire to control everything. Since Henry's release, I had been encouraging him to take a more active role in the household management. My brother-in-law suggested that putting something in Henry's name might encourage him to become more responsible.

Against my better judgment, I allowed the salesman to order a car that was specially built for Charlotte Johnson. Henry paid the money to secure the order. It took several weeks for the car to be built. During that time, I struggled with my decision. Henry had no plan to aid him in paying the car note. He just kept insisting that somehow, he would manage.

In the end, I gave him a plan to help him. He was working full time at a plant in Alabama. He could work with me part time to earn the money needed for the car and the additional insurance premium. This may have worked out well if someone hadn't been concerned about Henry getting enough sleep.

Be not deceived: evil communications corrupt good manners.
1 Corinthians 15:33

One Sunday evening, we were at home. Henry was in the bedroom, and I was in the den. When the telephone rang, we both answered. The person on the other end was so insistent that she never noticed that I answered the telephone.

As I walked down the hall, she went into a tirade. "Henry, did you get any sleep today? How much sleep did you get? Did you have to go to church today? I'M NOT GOING TO SAY ANYTHING! I know how to pray…."

By this time, I was standing in the doorway of the bedroom. Henry was looking up at me. He was barely commenting but the person on the other end never noticed. He knew this was vexing me. Finally, Henry broke the conversation.

Hating the conflict, he said, "CJ, do you want to say something? Annie, CJ's on the phone."

Calmly, I responded, "We answered the telephone at the same time. I'm standing in front of Buck, and he knows that I have been on the telephone since the beginning of this conversation. Are you praying against our marriage?"

When the conversation ended, I told Henry

what the Bible said about this interference. He tried to find a way to rationalize what had happened. He has a lot of respect for his sister. Yet, he didn't want me hurt or angry. He was trapped between right and wrong, leaving and cleaving.

In order for his car note and insurance to be paid on time, it was necessary for me to subsidize both. Henry would insist that he had given me enough money. To help him stay focused, I developed a budget sheet for him. Sacrificing for the car left Henry's budget extremely tight. Henry decided to remedy this problem.

I was angry and punished these greedy people. I withdrew myself from them but they went right on sinning.
Isaiah 57:17 NLT

Before trust was rebuilt, along came a little fudging or *a little white lie*. This went undetected. Then, there came a little deceit. Trust had never been reestablished. Deceitfulness has the potential to destroy any possibility of trust. The things that he took were insignificant in value. However, given our past experiences, they extracted a great price. Without his knowledge, **he risked everything for nothing.**

Henry was living better than he ever had. Not only was he looking good and smelling good, he had nice clothes. He was driving the car of his dreams. He had been working legally and consistently for more than a year. He was drug-free and crime free. He was reaching a point of successfully completing his parole and making the transition to probation.

If there arise among you a prophet, or a dreamer of dreams, and giveth thee a sign or a wonder, And the sign or the wonder come to pass, whereof he spake unto thee, saying, Let us go after other gods, which thou hast not known, and let us serve them; Thou shalt not hearken unto the words of that prophet, or that dreamer of dreams: for the LORD your God proveth you, to know whether ye love the LORD your God with all your *heart and with all your soul.*
Deuteronomy 13:1-3

Somebody whispered in his ear that he was working too hard. He wasn't getting enough sleep. He wasn't being treated fairly. He made the mistake of listening. He decided to equal things out. He felt justified in taking the things that he took. After all, he was using the funds for the household.

Woe unto them that rise up early in the morning, that they may follow strong drink; that continue until

night, till wine inflame them!
Isaiah 5:11

During the times when Henry was in his active addiction, Ms. Doll was the only person that called me to express concern for his sleeping habits. From the beginning of our relationship, I had worried about his welfare and his sleeping habits. There were times when he went days without sleeping. There were also times when his weight dropped rapidly because he wasn't eating properly. Darlene was the person who went with me into the streets at night to track him down. We wanted to make sure he got rest and nourishment. My children rode with me to track him down. They even learned how to track him down. Earline and LaToya had worked several hours one night to find a treatment facility to admit him.

For years, I had denied myself to assure he was as comfortable as possible during his incarcerations. Nothing was too good for him. After all, I was a good mother.

Now that he was attempting to do right by his family, there were those who dared to express concern for his wellbeing. At some point during the last twenty-two years, I'm sure that he could have used that concern. Nevertheless, he entertained their comments and began to feel that he was being treated unfairly.

Hell and destruction are never full;
so the eyes of man are

never satisfied.
Proverbs 27:20

When I began to suspect what he was doing, I didn't confront him. Rather than risking accusing him falsely, I set up checkpoints. Knowing that I was suspicious wasn't enough for him. This was the same pattern of behavior that led to his numerous incarcerations. He never knew when to quit. Henry continued his tricks. Finally, I set a trap for him. Even with knowing that I was attempting to trap him, he did it again. He tried to minimize what had happened.

His actions said that I had made another mistake. My finances needed to be put in order. Without hesitation, I secured all my investments. If at some point in the future, I discovered that I could trust my husband, I would reconsider the changes that I made.

Love is patient, love is kind. It does not envy, it does not boast, it is not proud. It is not rude, it is not self-seeking, it is not easily angered, it keeps no record of wrongs. Love does not delight in evil but rejoices with the truth. It always protects, always trusts, always hopes, always perseveres. Love never fails.
1 Corinthians 13:4-8 NIV

When love is not patient or enduring; when love is unforgiving and always disappointed... looking for something to go wrong, it generates fear in the other person. Fear-based love is conditional and creates an atmosphere of distrust, dishonesty and instability.

There is no fear in love. But perfect
love drives out fear because fear
has to do with punishment.
The one who fears is not made
perfect in love.
I John 4:18 NIV

We can have a limited trust in people as we grow to know them and they see that we really care about them. But the fact is that even the nicest person will let us down. That is a reality. God can claim to be perfectly faithful in everything but we can't. We will never be perfect and therefore, we will probably disappoint someone close to us at different times. We can make promises but the Bible says at some point we will fall short. This is not an excuse for us to actively practice a lifestyle of sin. Should we continue in sin? God forbid!

As it is written: "There is no one
righteous, not even one;
Romans 3:10

Trust is as fragile as a fine piece of porcelain. Whenever a person loses trust in their spouse, it's because the spouse has been untrustworthy; they have broken trust. It is like dropping the finest piece of porcelain. Trust is like that. Trust stands as a beautiful ornament in a marriage. We've committed ourselves to each other. We enter marriage trusting each other. Trust will remain until one or both partners become untrustworthy. When this occurs, trust will shatter into small pieces.

I hearkened and heard but they
spake not aright: no man repented
him of his wickedness, saying,
What have I done? every one turned
to his course, as the horse
rusheth into the battle.
Jeremiah 8:6

If the person will repent for what they've done and turn from their wrong, and then begin to live trustworthy again — that is doing what they say they're going to do — the ornament is glued back together. Trust will be reestablished in the marriage. If trust is violated a number of times, it's as if the porcelain ornament is shattered beyond repair. The porcelain is still there but you can no longer see the ornament. That often happens in a marriage where a person violates the trust of their spouse again and again. Whether it's the first time or many times, the only way for trust to be reborn is for the one who violated the trust to choose to be trustworthy. And consequently, change our lifestyle so that we are doing what we say we'll do.

One of the ways this happens is by giving the spouse evidence that we are now trustworthy. Trust will grow as the offending spouse demonstrates that they are going to be true to their word. The only way the trust can grow is for the person to have some evidence they're trustworthy. If we really are trustworthy if we've really changed and we'll be committed to our spouse, we should not object when they confirm we are doing what we said we would do. We should be glad because what they're doing is rebuilding trust in us.

Since I was sixteen years old, the bulk of the responsibility for my family has rested on me. It is difficult to imagine that things could ever be any other way. This does not just include those in my household. There are others who rely upon as a sort of surrogate mother. This creates a situation where I feel that I am constantly giving out of myself. There are times when I feel emotionally bankrupt because I'm not receiving what I am giving out. This creates a dangerous imbalance, which eventually has a volcanic effect. When I feel that I have had enough, I blow up. Usually, I get everybody at once. This is also a characteristic of co-dependency.

When trust has been violated, it is not easily restored. When the injured spouse is able to show the offending spouse a measure of God's grace, trust can be restored. The person who wants to be trusted must maintain a standard of trustworthiness. If the person continues to practice tricks of deceit, it will further impede the process of restoring trust to the relationship. If deceitful practices are foregoing for an extended period, it will be impossible to restore trust without the grace of God.

Without total submission to God, trust, honesty, thanksgiving, and grace, marriage is in danger of ending in betrayal or divorce. No marriage is perfect. That's because wherever there are two people, there tends to be imbalances. A couple needs a good sense of balance. Each of us has to go the extra mile, pull our fair share of the load, deal with dissatisfactions, let go of control, and share who we are. As we work toward balance in our marriage, we'll reap the rewards.

For they being ignorant of God's righteousness, and going about to establish their own righteousness, have not submitted themselves unto the righteousness of God.
Romans 10:3

When Henry decided this is mine and that is yours; he wanted to choose where to apply this principle. If this was going to be the guideline in our relationship, it was going to apply in every area. As in times past, I responded to what he did. This wasn't my usual volcanic explosion. It was by playing a game with him. He wanted everything in our relationship to be equal. The person conducting the measurement will always define the equality.

Equality is an utter impossibility in any relationship. All research is subject to manipulation, error, or flaws. Someone will always give more than the other will in some area. Where one spouse is weak the other should be strong. They should complement each other.

In my efforts to show him how ridiculous this game was, things got out of control. He was in a stage of rebellion. He was rebelling against Mama #2. He wasn't going to admit he had been wrong. He was committed to his course. I was just as committed. The game went on too long.

It was a dangerous and hurtful game. Do loving spouses hurt each other? **YES!** We still hurt each other and need confession and forgiveness in order to reconcile and keep our relationships healthy and loving. Forgiveness is one of the keys to trusting another fallible human being again.

Changing Old Habits

But to all who believed Him and accepted Him, He gave the right to become children of God. They are reborn! This is not a physical birth resulting from human passion or plan, this rebirth comes from God.

John 1:12-13 NLT

Our imagination can be a wonderful or a very destructive tool. It can inspire us to great feats and accomplishments. Our imagination can also cause great devastation and heartache. Worry begins with our imagination. It has been said that 90% of the things that we worry about never happen and the other 10% are things that we could do nothing to change.

Several years ago, Henry had a pair of blue jeans. I was particularly fond of the way they fit. One day, we were out shopping. This was during the Christmas holidays. While we shopped, I walked behind him. He preferred that I walk in front of him. Each time that he moved behind me, I reversed our positions.

Confused, he said, "I'm trying to make sure no one takes your purse. Stay in front of me!"

Laughingly, I replied, "I like the view from back here!"

This was confusing to him. Afterward I explained to him the power of imagination. He couldn't compete with my imagination. Whenever he wore these jeans, it was hard for me to stay angry with him. Every time something happened that he thought would vex me, he put the jeans on. This always worked. He wore them often. The jeans finally wore out. We searched diligently for another pair to no avail.

During a family vacation, we found a pair that was similar. The vacations were always shopping trips for me. Recently, I saw a friend wearing a pair of jeans. They made me think about Henry's jeans. I thought, "If Henry had those jeans we wouldn't be in this mess." He informed me that he had purchased them in Atlanta. I was tempted to drive to Atlanta to purchase a pair.

Every sinful habit in our lives gained its foothold through our thoughts and choices. We can gain victory over those habits by thinking God's thoughts. A person who feels unacceptable and unworthy can replace those negative feelings. The truth is that through Jesus, we have become worthy and acceptable. The process of conforming to the image of Jesus will be successful as we choose to replace negative thoughts with positive ones.

The way to change negative thinking is to choose to exchange the negative thought for its opposite. Our imaginations can help us see wonderful visions of the future. Before we can change our negative behaviors, we have to imagine ourselves being or doing something different.

Nevertheless, we have to add actions to our

thoughts. Without action, this becomes a dream induced by last night's dinner. If we can't imagine life being better, it will never be better.

Who hath put wisdom in the inward parts? or who hath given understanding to the heart?
Job 38:36

During the days when Henry and I were stealing, I had lots of clothes. In fact, I tried to wear a new outfit every day. Henry made sure that I had the outfits with matching stockings and shoes. In the days when we were selling drugs, he took me shopping every Sunday. Afterward he took me to a nice restaurant for dinner. As a result, I have always had more clothes than he has. He bought me leather jackets in every color. He bought me a blue fox coat. When I saw someone with one that was similar to mine, he sold the first coat and bought me a more expensive one. Yet, somehow, after his last release, Henry became concerned that I had more clothes than he has. What happened? The devil gained a foothold on his imagination.

He will give you all you need from day to day if you live for Him and make the Kingdom of God your primary concern.
Matthew 6:33 NLT

There was another thing that bothered him. When we were stealing, I always kept the money for our household. Henry kept the money that was for his drugs. I never gave him money to purchase drugs. When he was selling drugs, he gave the money to me for safe keeping. He kept a small amount of money for personal use.

Over the years, on more than one occasion, I spent the money that he put in my hands. Each time, the money was spent on the household. I have never squandered money. To keep him from blowing the money on drugs, I spent it. Yet, Henry began to complain that he needed to find a job. He said he needed money to shop. Working with me wasn't providing him enough money to shop at will.

Very few middle-class people are afforded this luxury. They work to provide for the families. Today, many people work more than one job. Some households have several incomes and yet they struggle with the upkeep of their household.

Henry actually had a lot of **things**. What happened? It started with his imagination. I had more **things** than he had. I had also been on the streets since 1987. During most of this time, I had a consistent income. Additionally, I hadn't used drugs since January of 1989. Even during my drug usage, shopping was a priority. This provided me an opportunity to acquire **things.**

"Trust in the LORD with all your heart and lean not on your own understanding; in all your ways

acknowledge Him, and He will make your paths straight. Do not be wise in your own eyes; fear the LORD and shun evil. This will bring health to your body and nourishment to your bones"
Proverbs 3:5-8 NLT

Before Henry returned home from prison, I made several critical decisions. I decided that this time, we would share everything. Considering his previous pattern of drug usage, this was a decision that I was uncomfortable with. Property in our relationship had always been ON one side. I always protected OUR interests. Trust had been broken in our relationship and it would have to be restored. Until this happened, I was not going to tell him about my FINANCIAL decisions or actions.

To make sure things were able to proceed according to my plan; I went to see his parole officer prior to his release. Henry had successfully completed his last two terms on parole. I assured him that he would complete this one. The problems usually occurred when he made the transition from parole to probation. He agreed to allow Henry to work and travel with me. When Henry went to see him for the first time, he gave him a hint of our previous conversation.

The officer stated, "You have been afforded an opportunity that very few inmates are able to walk into. I wonder if you know the opportunity that has been placed in your hands."

This should have given Henry a hint that something had changed in his favor. It should have spurred his imagination to think great thoughts and expectations. However, the truth was that he didn't know the opportunity that he had been provided. The 90% that was never going to happen took control of his thoughts. He worried that he wasn't being included.

As you may have read in *The Flip Side,* in 1986 Henry learned that I was a nag. The things that I nagged him about were never things to benefit me. They were things to help him change his lifestyle, stop the drug usage, and stay out prison. Most of all, I nagged him about his salvation. What changed? Again it was the thoughts triggered by his imagination.

In 1994, I began working a traditional job for the first time in a number of years. This was my first time working since meeting Henry. The Tally-Ho was an exception. Prior to this time, I drew disability. In every aspect, I was a housewife. Usually, I cooked every day. When I began working, this was no longer possible. My energy level just wouldn't permit it. This doesn't mean that I stopped cooking entirely. When Henry went to prison the last time, I stopped almost totally. When he returned home, I wanted to change this. However, I was working more than twelve hours a day. I had also grown accustomed to eating out. Again, his imagination went to work. He questioned my love for him.

There was another problem. Codependents are often manipulative and controlling. **I confess! I am guilty as charged!** Because he trusts and respects my judgment, some thought that he was henpecked. The Bible has instructed the husband to leave his family and cleave to his wife. When husbands begin to cleave to their wives they are often labeled as henpecked. In actuality, they are obeying the commandments of God. Although Henry is usually gentle and not prone to provoke confrontation, I would hardly call him henpecked. While he doesn't provoke confrontation, he doesn't run from one either.

Below are some jokes that I found about henpecked husbands. Based on these jokes, he is definitely not henpecked.

"A henpecked husband is a domestic animal trained to wash up and dry up but never to act up."

"The man who is afraid to think for himself usually chooses the wrong woman to think for him."

"Marriage brings out the animal in some men, usually the chicken."

"A henpecked husband is the only species of worm that's afraid to turn."

"The man who won't admit he's henpecked probably smokes a big cigar while washing the dishes."

The tricks of the imagination also caught me

in their clutches. When Henry was incarcerated, I often became lonely. I imagined what my life would be like if I had married someone from my past. Perhaps, my life would have been more normal. What's normal? Several of these dreams or illusions had to be put to rest. Thank God, it happened without me violating my marriage covenant.

Now the God of hope fill you with all
joy and peace in believing, that ye
may abound in hope, through the
power of the Holy Ghost.
Romans 15:13

The final illusion came in around **August 15, 2005.** For several days, people were bringing up Earline's father. This didn't bother me but I knew that Earline had unresolved issues with him. Finally, I contacted him. They needed to make peace. My conversation with him was very simple.

I came straight to the point, "This is Charlotte. Earline is on the telephone. She needs to talk to you. She's been a blessing to me. I'm getting off the phone."

I didn't wait for his response. Rather, I immediately hung up the telephone. Afterward I thought, "It would be nice to date him again, nice to have someone take me out to dinner and take me shopping."

When Henry came home from work, I decided to share what had happened with him. The telephone call was shared but not the thoughts of my imagination. He was in bed when I passed by him.

WITHOUT STOPPING TO EXPLAIN, I said, "We spoke to Earline's father today."

He responded, "What did you talk to him about?"

This was flattering. Although in recent weeks, I had been dressing to get his attention, he wouldn't verbalize a response. Henry is very particular about how I dress. His eyes said that I had hit the mark but there was a new emotion there, jealousy. He was struggling with the fact that I had been shopping without purchasing anything for him. His job wasn't supplying enough income for him to shop. It was his choice to work with the temporary service rather than working with me. Flattered that I had finally gotten a response from him, I laughed.

He was not amused; "I don't have a right to ask?"

For several days, I entertained my thoughts about Earline's father. However, I didn't act on them. My imagination was playing tricks with me. These were never things that we did together. They were things that I did with Henry.

Wisdom is to do now what we will be satisfied with later. I made the mistake of not responding to his question. Henry's imagination went to work again. His imagination played terrible tricks on him. He decided to make some contacts of his own. He took it further than I did. He made ungodly choices. These choices have negative consequences. Bad habits returned. Perhaps, they had never been broken.

Therefore hear now this, thou afflicted, and drunken but not with wine: Thus saith thy Lord the LORD, and thy God that pleadeth the cause of His people, Behold, I have taken out of thine hand the cup of trembling, even the dregs of the cup of My fury; thou shalt no more drink it again:
Isaiah 51:21-22

Henry's sly actions indicated that he couldn't be trusted. He began coming in late. On more than one occasion, I was concerned that he had picked up his old habits. One Sunday night, he came in extremely late. He had gone to church earlier in the day but didn't come directly home. This was in mid-**September 2005**. His lips were greased. He was also twitching them in a way that was very familiar to me. There were other outward signs that were familiar. This was pushing things too far. I knew that a separation was imminent. The car was still in my name and I was concerned about this. I didn't want to keep this car.

Henry had also started on a different path.

He was proud to tell me on a number of occasions that he was handling his own business. Even when his business involved me, he was determined to resolve it without my knowledge or help. This led to him having a small legal complication. This was totally unnecessary. He had a warning. He needed my help to resolve it. He needed information from me but we weren't communicating. That was his excuse for failing to ask me for the needed information.

Refusing to talk to me, he handled it on his own. It was his business. In the end, I was forced to repair the damage. The legal entities refused to believe that I had no knowledge of what had happened. They were nasty and exaggerated the incident. They doubled his fine, and I was forced to pay it. Even with this, he wanted to check behind me. His interference would have made things worse. His insistence led to my losing it again. The magic words came forth; **"I'm filing for a divorce."**

First, we needed to get the car out of my name. Originally, I added his name as a cosigner to the loan. This was only to help him build his credit. After a year, we would attempt to get the car refinanced in his name. It had been less than a year.

Henry continued to come home at whatever time he deemed appropriate. It was disrespectful and inconsiderate. On more than one occasion, I started to reach out to him and resolve the problems in our relationship. Stubbornness said no.

How beautiful on the mountains are
the feet of those who bring good

news of peace and salvation!
Isaiah 52:7 NLT

When I thought about all the times that I had taken the initiative to resolve our differences, **I decided** that it was time for him to take the leadership. He was standing his ground. He wasn't going to apologize. The house was a strange place to live. Without communication between us, I felt drained. The strain was affecting everything in my life. It felt hypocritical to help other people when my own house was in turmoil. There seemed to be no end in sight. Each time Henry came in late, I became more agitated. This had been going on too long; it needed to end. Peace needed to return to the house. If we ended the marriage, everything would return to normal. That's what I thought at the time!

With reservations, I made an appointment for us to go to the credit union. It was almost two months early but maybe the loan would go through. There were several things that needed to be corrected with his credit. With the conflict in our relationship, they had been neglected. Based on all the circumstances, it was unlikely that the loan was going to be approved. At any rate, I knew there were no guarantees.

The car had become an obsession for Henry. He was so in love with the car that he didn't even want my Bible to ride in the car. It was going to be embarrassing if he wasn't allowed to purchase the car from me. This was weighing heavily on me. If the financing wasn't approved, it would leave me with the car and the car note. There were no easy answers. Henry was not going to give the car up easily.

After contemplating this for several days, I decided to take the keys from Henry. I also decided that he needed to move out. It was the first day of the month. Financially, this seemed to be a good breaking point. It would keep additional bills from accumulating that I would later be stuck with. We could meet at the credit union to sign the papers and make the transfer.

After I took the keys, I discovered Henry had another plan. He had also made an appointment with the credit union. He planned to go without me. He said he didn't need me to go; he was handling his own business. He was planning to get in **his car** and ride off. It was hard for me to understand how he planned to buy the car from me without me being there. With a lot of insisting from me, Henry moved out that night.

That Monday, he went to the credit union without me. He instructed the loan officer not to talk to me about the transaction. When he ran into trouble with the financing, he called me for help. He needed a two-thousand-dollar down payment. He didn't have it and wanted me to help him with the money or let the car remain in my name. He had already been given the second option. His loan officer was adamant; he told her not to discuss the transaction with me. This was awkward. Originally, I had never planned to tell her about our separation.

My family had been transacting business with her for years. His greatest asset was his marriage to me. He handled his own business, and he suffered the consequences. When he couldn't resolve the issues with the car, he blamed me.

This left me stuck with the car, a car I didn't desire. My fears were hitting home. It had been a mistake from the beginning. That car had only caused me grief. I felt trapped. It was for the best that he wasn't approved for the car. It would have been hard for me to accept another woman riding in the car with him, a car built especially for *Charlotte Johnson.* Even the thought of it made the old Charlotte rise.

A Ministry of Grace

But rise, … I have appeared unto thee for this purpose, to make thee a minister … of these things which thou hast seen, and of those things in the which I will appear unto thee; … unto whom now I send thee, To open their eyes, … unto God,

Acts 16:16-18a

Grace is God's loving, active presence in the world. Grace is usually defined as unmerited favor. Another way to express this is to contrast it with mercy. Mercy is God withholding what we deserve; grace is God giving us what we don't deserve. Grace is the free favor of God by which He has in Christ provided the way for our salvation. He has enabled us to embrace Christ.

When I think about myself, I can only describe myself as a product of GRACE, God's Amazing Grace. I live in place beyond Faith called Grace. My life, my ministry, and my very existence are based on grace. In *Grace Under Fire*, I stated that except for the grace of God there was going to be another divorce. We were already taking each other for granted. Pride was causing interference in our marriage. Pride can hinder any relationship. Wrath can brew to the point of destroying a relationship or a family. When either party in a relationship has obvious difficulty accepting or acknowledging faults or mistakes, a crisis looms on the horizon. When apologies are slow to come, wrath continues to brew.

My frustration had grown for months. Outside forces were also causing interference in our marriage. I was tired of the years of struggle. It would have been easy for me to take the initiative to resolve our conflicts. The conflicts were actually minor. Instead of resolving our conflicts, I stilled my heart towards him. This was easy. Each time I spoke to him, he was defensive. There was an edge in his voice.

And if a woman shall put away her
husband, and be married to another,
she committeth adultery.
Mark 10:12

The time to take the final decree for our third divorce was drawing near. I had tried to schedule the date for two weeks. There was a conflict in the judge's schedule that prevented this. In the interim, I tried to focus on the things that were wrong in our relationship. It was working.

Then something happened. Henry called me. Perhaps, he wishes that he had never made that telephone call. He wanted to explain to me the status of our divorce. It was almost funny. This was my fourth time going through this process. Even without the previous experience, it was unlike me to leave loose ends untied. On numerous occasions, I had resolved legal issues for him.

I thank Thee, and praise? Thee, O
Thou God of my fathers, who hast
given me wisdom and might, and
hast made known unto me now
what we desired of Thee: for
Thou hast now made known
unto us the king's matter.
Daniel 2:23

During his phone call, I was polite and formal. Afterward I felt bad about it. This wasn't a stranger that I was speaking to. He was my husband. I called him back to apologize. We had our first decent conversation in months. When the conversation ended, I was still committed to taking the final decree. However, I forgot to guard my heart. During the night, God began to prick my heart.

The next morning, my mother accompanied me to the courthouse. Mild uncertainty began to grip my heart. When we arrived outside the courtroom, there was another delay. This had always been a quick procedure. The bailiff asked us to wait outside the courtroom. We waited for more than an hour. As we waited, one statement kept repeating in my mind

"Except for the grace of God, there will be another divorce."

The more we waited, the more the statement hit close to home. If I followed through with the divorce, was I saying the grace of God was not sufficient? I couldn't rationalize grace. God had brought me through too many seemingly impossible situations. Finally, I told my mother what I was thinking. She didn't hesitate to answer.

Sternly, she said, "If you are not sure what to do, don't do anything!"

And He said unto me, My grace is sufficient for thee: for My strength is made perfect in weakness. Most gladly therefore will I rather glory in my infirmities, that the power of Christ may rest upon me.
2 Corinthians 12:9

For another forty-five minutes, I tried to ignore my thoughts. I tried to do it **my way**. Whenever we attempt to do it our way, rather than **His way**, we are destined for trouble. God is always waiting for us to ask for His help and instruction. We both knew that we needed help. Yet, we refused to ask for it.

What keeps us repeating the mistakes of the past, when the answer is within our reach? After going back and forth several times, I was standing on the outside of the courthouse. The temptation to rush back into the courthouse was great. In the end, I walked away. I didn't know why God had not allowed me to go through with the divorce.

Whether He is dealing with nations or individuals, God the Father always thinks Grace.

Whether He is exercising His divine justice, wrath, love, or mercy, He thinks Grace. The Grace of God influences all His thoughts and actions.

Mastery of the Bible's teaching about Grace is the most important goal of Christian living. The following are some of the reasons why the subject of Grace is so important to every Christian:

- Grace is the most important single concept in the Word of God.
- Salvation is "by Grace through faith"
- The Christian way of life functions entirely on Grace Principles.
- Knowledge of Grace Principles gives the believer knowledge and confidence in God's plan, provisions, and blessings.
- Grace gives Christians insight into God's intentions regarding the future.
- Grace convinces Christians that human righteousness is completely unacceptable.

We are all debtors to others and to society as a whole. We often feel that people owe us many things in our human relationships. We feel we are owed courtesy and consideration. Sometimes, we think that we are owed a reward or status or a promotion.

What should a Christian do about all of the debts owed to him? Answer: **forgive** them, as Christ forgave us. A Christian who practices Grace thinking will become a forgiving person. To forgive means "to give up a claim; to cease bearing resentment".

As the day continued, God began to deal with me about my heart. Bitterness and resentment had begun to build in my heart against Henry. For years, I had supported and encouraged him, stood by him, and loved him. In exchange, I had often received ingratitude and infidelity. Although I wanted to forgive him, I hadn't. Divorcing him would have been for the wrong reasons.

Jesus said that if we do not forgive others that have hurt and damaged us, God would not forgive us. Unforgiveness, resentment and using the sins committed against us, as a justification of our own sinful reactions is not an option for a Christian. The love of God should shine through every child of God.

Grace means that man has received from God that which he has not earned or deserved. Nothing that we are and nothing that we have is sufficient to qualify us for any of what the Lord gives to us or does for us.

Now therefore, I pray Thee if I have found grace in Thy sight, shew me now Thy way, that I may know Thee, that I may find grace in Thy sight: and consider that this nation is Thy people.
Exodus 33:13

As new Christians grow in Christ, they learn to "think Grace" rather than thinking pride. They think Grace in times of doubt, in times of poverty, in times of prosperity, in suffering and pressure, and even in the midst of persecution. The new believer has only "tasted Grace". Grace is the most outstanding quality of the mature believer in Christ.

Grace is a God-given advantage and benefit. Without Christ, there is no mercy, love or grace. There is only hopelessness, wrath, judgment, and condemnation. I wanted to take this position. However, God in His infinite wisdom would not allow this. There was too much at stake. I have claimed to be a representative of Him. As such, I have given up my natural rights to accept my God-given rights. The mature Christian is gracious, forgiving, and unassuming. He is uplifting and encouraging, not depressing. Out of his innermost being flows a river of living water. He is a conduit that brings the Grace of God to a dying world.

Now that I had decided not to follow through with the divorce, Henry needed to be told about my decision. I was not looking forward to giving him this news.

The opposite of grace is pride. A symptom of pride is unforgiveness, the holding of grudges. Pride prevents a forgiving attitude. How many marriages break up because of this? Grace thinking overcomes pride, and the symptoms of sinful pride will start to disappear. A person who was at first totally filled with pride will find that as he grows in Christ, the symptoms will seldom show up. Unconfessed sin leads the believer away from Christ. We must know who and what God is so that we will not hesitate to believe that He can do what He has promised to do.

God never condones divorce. However, He is willing to assist us through the process. Perhaps, it's praying to know the right timing of the divorce itself. Perhaps, it's deciding which spouse will actually file for the divorce or who will physically stay in the house and who will leave.

Pride ends in humiliation, while
humility brings honor.
Proverbs 29:23 NLT

We need to pray with the right motives. We need to have forgiveness in our heart toward our spouses. We need daily direction from God for all major decisions both before and after the final separation. Most importantly, we need to receive the cleansing that God wants to do in our own heart so we won't repeat old sins and behaviors of the past. We need to grow in grace and be changed into His likeness. God wants to direct every area of our life.

In all your ways acknowledge Him,
and He shall direct [ALL] your paths
Proverbs 3:6

We need the Spirit of God during a divorce to leave us free and at peace. When we allow our feelings to lead us, we will not be at peace or rest. On the contrary, we may be legally divorced but we will still be bound by unforgiveness, resentment, anger and blame. Additionally, we may still be bound to our spouses emotionally. Any divorce is futile when both parties retain the love for their spouse. I had tried this way twice. This was a mistake that I didn't want to repeat.

Grace can be found all around us, among us, and within us. God constantly touches our lives, attempting to reach us through other people, places, events, and the material things we encounter every day. He loves us in spite of ourselves. It is our sins that He hates.

For by grace you have been saved
through faith, and that not of
yourselves; it is the gift of God;
not as a result of works,
that no one should boast
Ephesians 2:8-9 NLT

There is nothing we can do to earn God's favor. We are unable to please Him enough to be given His blessings. We certainly could never pay for our own sins and be saved. Grace in the form of love gives. It gives and demands nothing in return. God's grace is sufficient to save the most wretched sinner and the most troubled marriage.

Psalm 70

NLT

For the choir director: A psalm of David, to bring us to the Lord's remembrance.

Please, God, rescue me! Come
quickly, LORD, and help me.
May those who try to destroy me
be humiliated and put to shame.
May those who take delight in my
trouble be turned back in disgrace.

Let them be horrified by their
shame, for they said, "Aha! We've got
him now!"

But may all who search for You
be filled with joy and gladness.
May those who love Your salvation
repeatedly shout, "God is great!"

But I am poor and needy;
please hurry to my aid, O God.
You are my helper and my savior;
O LORD, do not delay!

Ice Cold

Now a thing was secretly brought to me, and mine ear received a little thereof. In thoughts from the visions of the night, when deep sleep falleth on men, Fear came upon me, and trembling, which made all my bones to shake.
Job 4:12-14

Even thinking about talking to Henry was difficult. There were no answers. My intentions were not to reconcile the relationship. Honestly, I didn't have any intentions. I didn't know if the next week I would be able to follow through with the divorce. The only thing that I was certain of was that God wanted to talk to me. It would be easier to let someone else relay the message to Henry. After I was unable to reach the person that I had in mind, I made the dreaded telephone call.

When I told him that I had been unable to follow through with the divorce, he was shocked and agitated. He shouldn't have been shocked. It wasn't the first time I had reacted hastily out of frustration. It wasn't the first time that God had rebuked me for my behavior. He knew that once God convicted me of something, there was no way that I was going to ignore Him. He had no right to be angry or agitated. Henry had not contributed to the divorce. He had no financial investment in the outcome.

The drama was supposed to be over. At least, that was what I thought. Rather than focusing on Henry or his response, I began searching for answers. As the days went by, God began to deliver me from resentment, anger, revenge, and unforgiveness. All were emotions that I was familiar with. They were also emotions that I thought I had overcome. Surely, I had forgiven Henry for his relationship with Sister Juanita. He continuously apologized for the relationship. I didn't doubt his sincerity. The relationship had served to break a stronghold in his life. Before his relationship with Sister Juanita, he had roving eyes. He no longer has this problem.

He that is slow to anger is better than the mighty; and he that ruleth his spirit than he that taketh a city.
Proverbs 16:32

What was God saying to me? It had taken years for me stop trusting Henry. A little hurt here, a little hurt there, a little neglect here, a little neglect there, a rumor here, a rumor there, when it all got together, it made a big pile. It made a pile of resentment. My actions were based on emotions that God was not pleased with. More than dealing with the marriage, He wanted to deal with me.

Blessed are the undefiled in the way, who walk in the law of the LORD. Blessed are they that keep His testimonies, and that seek Him

with the whole heart.
Psalm 119:1-2

It wasn't hard for me to recognize my folly. **My will** was put aside and I decided to wait for God-given direction. Too many mistakes had already been made.

"Oh, the tangled webs we weave
when first we practice to deceive!"

Approximately two weeks later, someone approached me. They shared information with me that almost sent me into shock.

"He's living in Alabama with his first wife, Varetta. They were living with Annie, his sister but now they have moved down the street. She was down there before the separation. When he was living with you, he was going down there to visit her. Marjorie says that you and he were never married."

I later discovered that he had moved to Auburn, Alabama, a town near his sister, Annie. His ex-wife was living with him.

It is not merely knowing the law that
brings God's approval. Those who
obey the law will be declared
right in God's sight.
Romans 2:13 NLT

This was a shock that I can't explain. It

chilled me to my bones. I felt ice cold. His sister had been a professing Christian for years. She was also a close friend of Sister Juanita. It was hard to believe any Christian woman would consent to this arrangement.

Earline responded, **"If I had known calling my father was going to trigger all this, I never would have called him!"**

This was something that I couldn't even respond to. There had to be a mistake. Who would allow such a thing? No saint that I knew would uphold such foolishness. Several emotions hit me at once, shock and disbelief, and then humor. It was almost ridiculous. Henry and I had been involved for almost twenty-two years. During the last fifteen years, I doubt if he had mentioned Varetta three times. This happened during times that he was explaining to me how stupid it would be to rekindle a relationship with someone from my past. I rushed home to call Annie.

There had to be a mistake. Surely, this wasn't something that she would take part in. She knows the Word of God. The information had to be wrong. Sister Annie wouldn't uphold such an open disrespect for the word. She wouldn't jeopardize her own reputation. Most importantly, she wouldn't jeopardize her own relationship with Christ by upholding someone else's sin. At least, this was my assumption. The facts had to be wrong.

Do not nurse hatred in your heart
for any of your relatives." Confront
your neighbors directly so you will

not be held guilty for their crimes.
Leviticus 19:17 NLT

When I got home, I placed the call to my sister-in-law. Before assuming the validity of this information, I needed to give her an opportunity to explain. When she answered the telephone, I searched for the appropriate words. I didn't want to accuse her of such a treacherous sin.

Very politely, I asked, "If I ask you something, will you give me an honest answer?"

Hesitantly, she responded, "Well... What is it you want to ask me?"

There was no way around it. My next question would have to be more direct. She was being careful with her answers.

Without hesitation, I asked, "When was the last time that you saw Vet?"

Evasively, she answered, "Why would you ask me something like that?"

She never answered my question, so I shared with her the information that had been given to me. I also assured her that my marriage to Henry was indeed legal. His divorce from Varetta had been final for almost twenty years. Any relationship that they were having is, in fact, adulterous. She never confirmed or denied her involvement. Instead, she asserted her confidence in Henry's salvation.

She repeated several times, "I know God has done something for Henry. He's praying and reading his Bible. He obeys the Word."

And have no fellowship with the unfruitful works of darkness but rather reprove them. For it is a shame even to speak of those things which are done of them in secret. But all things that are reproved are made manifest by the light: for whatsoever doth make manifest is light.

Ephesians 5:11-13

On several occasions, I had called her home asking to speak to Henry. More than once, she had indicated she didn't know exactly where he was. She lives in a small mobile home. It was impossible for her to be unaware of who was in the home with her. To give her a second chance, to be honest, I asked another direct question

I asked her, "Does Henry still live with you?"

She responded, "Henry is over here all the time?"

Again, she avoided answering the question. Her attitude shocked me. Was it possible that what I had heard was true? Her involvement surprised me more than Henry's. For years, I had known his commitment to Christ was shaky. However, Annie was confessing salvation when I met her. Even at that time, she wasn't considered a new convert. That was more than twenty years ago. Hopefully, with the passing of time, we grow more like Christ. Henry had so much faith in her that I assumed he was correct; she was a devout Christian.

This then is the message which we have heard of Him, and declare unto you, that God is light, and in Him is no darkness at all. If we say that we have fellowship with Him, and walk in darkness, we lie, and do not the truth: But if we walk in the light, as He is in the light, we have fellowship one with another, and the blood of Jesus Christ His Son cleanseth us from all sin.
1 John 1:5-7

There are some things that a new convert would detest. Similarly, some people who claim no relationship with Christ would find this immoral. Even when I was openly practicing sin, I knew right from wrong and good from evil. It's a meticulous choice to do wrong or evil. When I made those choices, I never called them good or godly. If I had chosen to justify my sins, I would still be trapped by my sinful lifestyle.

The next day, I ordered a copy of Henry's final divorce decree from Varetta. When I received the confirmation email that the final divorce decree had been located, I forwarded an email copy to Annie. Later, I decided to visit Henry at his job.

After confirming that he was scheduled to work that day, I decided to meet him as his shift was terminating. With me, I carried a copy of the email. It was relatively easy for me to locate his new car in the parking lot. I parked across from it and waited for him to exit the factory. It was early morning when he came out of the plant. He was startled to see me. He was also concerned for my safety.

As we stood next to his car, I came to the point. I knew what had triggered his actions but I didn't want to accuse him. At this point, he was not going to admit the truth. Thinking that I was involved with a former lover had given him the same idea.

"But I tell you that anyone who divorces his wife, except for marital unfaithfulness, causes her to become an adulteress, and anyone who marries the divorced woman commits adultery."
Matthew 5:32 NIV

Looking directly into his eyes, I told him, "I have not been unfaithful to my marriage vows, not even in a conversation."

He responded, "Why are you telling me this?"

This was something that he needed to know. He understood exactly why I was telling him this. Denial wasn't going to allow him to admit the truth. If, I understood anything, I understood that. There had been too many of these conversations.

This wasn't the first time that he had mimicked my behavior. In his conversations with other people, he often repeated my thoughts as if they were his own. Usually, it was some scriptural lesson that I was trying to convey to him. During our conversations, he would remain silent or disagree with me. Later, he would enthusiastically share this information in conversations with someone else. These conversations occurred on a regular basis. Since his return from the last incarceration, this was part of the problem in our relationship. However, I didn't recognize the depth of the problem.

For my love they are my adversaries:
but I give myself unto prayer.
Psalm 109:4

Henry was provided with a copy of the email. Then he gave me something. It was another shock. This served to convince me that I was indeed having a bad nightmare. I told myself that I would wake up soon. He was assured of the accuracy of his information.

He looked into my eyes and said, "But, we have never been married." It was difficult for me to contain my laughter, so I didn't.

"You mean that we have been married in three different counties, by two justice of the peace, and two preachers, (once was a renewal of our vows) and we aren't married? If anybody is married, we are!"

Determined to convince me, he asserted, "No, seriously! I called the government center and the lady told me that we were never married. You need to call down there and talk to her."

"Did she know how many times we have been married? What did you tell her? Did you tell her that we were married in three different counties?"

"She knew all of that. I'm telling you, you need to call down there! Let Annie know what you find out," Henry replied.

Later that morning, I decided to placate him by calling the courthouse. This was a three-way call with Annie on the other line. When I explained the reason for my call to the clerk, I'm sure that she thought I had lost my mind.

Puzzled, she asked, "Who told you to call? And they said ask what?"

Laughing, I responded, "My husband told me to call."

Still puzzled, she said, "Well, I have the license in my hand. You said who told you to call?"

I will be faithful to you and make
you mine, and you will finally
know Me as LORD.
Hosea 2:20

The certified copies of the divorce decree arrived about a week later. I mailed Henry and Annie copies of it. Additionally, I took Marjorie and Darlene a copy. Henry didn't respond to this information. He preferred to communicate with me through Annie. After she continued being cagey in her communications and cloaking for his behavior, I decided to discontinue the telephone calls. I wasn't angry with her but I didn't want to add to the things she needed to repent for.

When I thought about our situation, I felt a variety of emotions and feelings. Anger wasn't one of them. I thought: this is funny. It was one of the craziest things that I had ever heard of. However, God never finds sin funny. I thought we certainly have come full circle. I had slept with Varetta's husband; now, she's sleeping with mine. Yet, God never winks at sin. I thought: this is poetic justice. Nevertheless, God doesn't measure justice the way that we do. I thought: this is so pathetic that I feel sorry for my husband. Nonetheless, God never excuses sin. I thought: Lord please, help my **poor** husband. Actually, for months He had been trying to get Henry's attention.

There were times when I felt sad. At other times, I felt betrayed. There were even times that I felt lonely. At times, I felt used and violated. There were even times that I felt relieved. But more than anything else, I felt ice cold. It chilled me to my very bones. I wondered if I would ever be warm again.

Warmer Days

No Harm… No Offense…

No harm meant to be given…
No offense should be taken…
If I knew better…
I'd do better…
This is just the way we do this thang…
Where I come from…

I was an addict before I was born…
I see nothing wrong with a lil' porn…
What's wrong with a life of crime?
I can do the time…
No harm meant to be given…
No offense should be taken…

You're related to me…
Sex with you should be free…
He's still blessing me…
He knows what they say about me…
If I knew better…
I'd do better…

My family supports my lies…
It's in sin that I thrive…
You owe me…
It's an entitlement, you see…
This is just the way we do this thang…
Where I come from…

I'll receive no harm...
I'll take no offense...
If you knew better...
You would do better...
This isn't the way we do it...
Where I come from...

Addict, you can be reborn...
You can be delivered from porn...
Change your criminal mind...
Before it's everlasting time...
Your harm has been given...
Offense has been taken...

I'm your cousin can't you see...
Sex with me should never be...
His blessings are always free...
It doesn't matter who you happen to be...
I'm telling you better...
Now do better...

Break free of your family's lies...
It's time that sin dies...
He knows how to pay...
If you continue to play...
This is the way He does it...
Where I come from!!!

No Harm... No Offense...

"No harm meant to be given, no offense should be taken; this is just the way we do it where I come from."

When you follow the desires of your sinful nature, your lives will produce these evil results: sexual immorality, impure thoughts, eagerness for lustful pleasure,
Galatians 5:19 NLT

A number of years ago, I heard a minister offering advice to his congregation. This sermon was directed primarily at the singles, as it was a little late for most of the married couples.

"Before you marry someone, you need to know something about their families. You might be marrying someone with a lunatic in their family. You have the potential of having a lunatic child."

While on some level, this may have been comical, it bears a great deal of truth. Through our families, we learn the basics of relationships. However, we sometimes develop strategies to help us cope with difficult or "dysfunctional" family situations such as parents who are critical, abusive, controlling, drug addicts or alcoholics.

Recently, I observed a young couple at the mall. For more than an hour, they engaged in verbal conflict. Finally, it escalated to a point that they were yelling obscenities about each other's families. In the young girl's arm was a young baby that bore an amazing resemblance to the young man. Based on their vulgar descriptions of each other's families, they could have benefited from this pastor's advice a year earlier.

For many couples, arguments are especially hard to resolve because of the things they learned from their families about arguing and resolving disagreements. Some learned to get very angry quickly and then get over it quickly. Others learned that yelling is a sign that things are very serious. Others learned very little about expressing themselves when they disagree and find they aren't sure what to say or do.

Idolatry, participation in demonic activities, hostility, quarreling, jealousy, outbursts of anger, selfish ambition, divisions, the feeling that everyone is wrong except those in your own little group, envy, drunkenness, wild parties, and other kinds of sin. Let me tell you again, as I have before, that anyone living that sort of life will not inherit the Kingdom of God.
Galatians 5:20-21 NLT

In some families, children are apprenticed into a life of crime. From an early age, they are taught how to watch for policemen. Some children are taught to hide stolen merchandise and drugs. Other children are taught to accept money from men beginning at a young age. Those who are viewed as grandfathers may later become intimate with the teenage child. The family does not view this as child molestation because the child has grown accustomed to receiving the financial benefits.

My mother would never have knowingly participated in my illegal activities. However, in some families, crime is excused based on racial inequality, economic hardship, or a sense of entitlement. They view crime as a necessity for those who refuse to avail themselves to the educational and training opportunities that are readily available. Paramours are exchanged throughout the family.

Another family may view as repulsive what one family may find acceptable or normal. When two people from very different backgrounds enter a relationship, the potential for conflict is high. When one person respects or overly values the opinion of someone in the family, it can lead to a crisis. The respected member of the family may not provide Biblically sound advice. A young man recently shared this story with me.

"She was telling me all kind of negative things about my wife. (Referring to a close family member who professes to be a Christian) She was sowing seeds of discord. When I began to pray, I discovered her motives weren't pure. She was trying to exercise control over my life and pull me away from my wife. If I had accepted her advice, it would have torn me away from the most stable relationship in my life. My wife is a gift to me from God. I would have been a fool to pull away from my blessing."

And be not drunk with wine,
wherein is excess; but be
filled with the Spirit;
Ephesians 5:18

When I was released from jail in 1984 after serving two weeks, I walked to my mother's house in Warren Williams Apartments. On the way, I stopped for a beer. When I arrived at her house, I finished the contents of the can before entering the house. It had never been acceptable for me to do certain things in her presence. There was a trashcan next to her porch. Before entering the apartment, this was where I disposed of the can. Mama was going to drive me back to my apartment. As we were leaving her apartment, she put something in the trashcan. She discovered my beer can. She instructed me to remove the can and further stated that the can could not ride in her car. The next door neighbor allowed me to dispose of the can in her trash can.

In those days Israel had no king, so
the people did whatever seemed
right in their own eyes.
Judges 21:25

In some families, it's acceptable for parents and children to abuse alcohol and drugs together. Substance abuse is the norm. For some it is acceptable for a first or second cousin to engage in an incestuous relationship. There would be nothing abnormal about a cousin being the mistress of a cousin. Adultery is openly practiced in many circles and even encouraged. One person may openly engage in sexual relationships with several members of one family and several close friends. In some families, career criminals are the successful and respected members. When their actions cause harm or offense to others, it's not intentional. It's nothing personal against you. They would do the same to anybody, friends, long-term family members, neighbors, and church members. This is just the way it's done in their family.

That night some of the leaders
of Gibeah surrounded the house,
planning to kill me, and they raped
my concubine until she was dead. So
I cut her body into twelve pieces
and sent the pieces throughout the
land of Israel, for these men
have committed this terrible
and shameful crime.
Judges 20:5-6 NLT

Once, I gave a ride to someone in my car. They were not allowed to smoke or drink alcoholic beverages in the car. This person was confused by my rigidness.

They responded, "My sister lets me drink on her porch. She's a Christian. I can't drink in the house but she knows that I have to have my liquor."

Some Christians have more liberal values than others do. For some Christians, the rules or their interpretation of sin changes when it involves a family member. For them, the original sin can be corrected if you change your actions later. For some, even adulterous relationships are condoned if you can get it straight quickly by divorcing your spouse. It is even permissible to interfere with a person's marital relationship.

Similarly, teach the older women to live in a way that is appropriate for someone serving the Lord. They must not go around speaking evil of others and must not be heavy drinkers. Instead, they should teach others what is good.
Titus 2:3 NLT

Some professing Christians demonstrate by their open disrespect for God's Word a belief that God's commandments change based on convenience. While they observe those close to them openly practicing sin, they continue to insist that God is blessing the sinner and the sinner is growing closer to Him. They may encourage the person to commit another sin to correct the previous sin, assuming that in doing so they will secure the blessings of God. The person or persons encouraging the sin may assume they will be held blameless for partaking in the sinful acts of others. Shall we continue in sin that grace may abound? God forbid! These things should not be once named among the saints.

In my family, it would never be acceptable to have sexual relationships with anyone but a spouse. This is not to say that it doesn't happen. However if it does, you don't engage in the act in the home of someone else. In other words, you are on your own. Don't expect help. You don't take it to the home of a family member. It would be unacceptable for me to ask my mother for permission to do so. My mother would never allow my former spouse or boyfriend to move into her home. If an emergency occurred that required temporary emergency housing, she would not have condoned hiding this information from my spouse. I wouldn't be allowed to meet my paramour at her home. It would also be unacceptable for me expect my mother to condone my sins. The Bible doesn't change its commandments because I'm her child. My marital relationship is off limits. This is normal for my family. For other families, adultery and fornication are acceptable behaviors.

Some families are loving and supportive. They applaud the success of each individual. Education and financial stability are encouraged. Salvation and loyalty are encouraged. In other families, individuals are encouraged to pursue negative or illegal behaviors. For them, the person who attempts to escape the destructive patterns of the family is ostracized. Rather than risking being ridiculed by the family, the person may choose to return to a previously acceptable role in the family.

In some families, it is acceptable to curse and belittle children. There are four basic roles that children adopt in order to survive growing up in emotionally dishonest, shame-based, dysfunctional families. Most emotional problems and difficulties are the result of individuals being raised in dysfunctional families.

For in many things we offend all. If
any man offend not in word, the
same is a perfect man, and able
also to bridle the whole body.
James 3:2

The essence of a dysfunctional family is that the parents were unable to meet the emotional needs of their children. A dysfunctional family is an unhealthy place where family members adopt destructive behaviors in order to cope with pain, abuse, suffering, poverty, fear and loneliness. The parents often express a shaming attitude towards their children. Children may be called crazy, stupid, retarded, gay, or queer. As a result, children grow up out of touch with their feelings, thoughts, and needs. They may even adopt these identities. It is not uncommon for children to experience verbal, emotional, physical, and sexual abuse.

Alcoholic and chemically dependent families

are prime breeding grounds for emotional problems. Children adopt roles to fit into these families. Some children maintain one role into adulthood while others switch from one role to another as the family dynamics changes. We adapt the roles that are best suited to our personalities.

"Adjuster" - "Lost Child"

This child escapes by attempting to be invisible. They daydream, fantasize, read a lot of books, play video games continuously, or watch a lot of television. They deal with reality by withdrawing from it. They deny that they have any feelings and "don't bother getting upset." They appear to be well-behaved because they require little attention. This child's needs often go unmet because they do not express their feelings. They may not feel that their needs will be met or that their feelings are important. It is not uncommon for this child to romanticize their life and wait to be rescued.

Earline dealt with the dysfunction in our family by reading countless books. She never asked for much. Earline constantly watched television. She often read the dictionary and the encyclopedias. She was often more advanced than her peers. This allowed her free time at school. This time was spent in the library.

Once, Earline was given an academic achievement test. She was in the second or third grade. One of the questions asked what an ameba was. Earline answered the question. The teacher wanted to know how Earline acquired this information. To this she replied that she read about it in the dictionary.

These children grow up to be adults who find themselves unable to feel and suffer very low self-esteem. They are also terrified of intimacy and often have relationship phobia. They are very withdrawn and shy and become socially isolated because that is the only way they know to be safe from being hurt. A lot of actors and writers are 'lost children' who have found a way to express emotions while hiding behind their characters. Most authors are shy or introverted.

"Acting out child" - "Scapegoat"

This is the child that the family feels ashamed of. They may become drug addicts, rapists, child molesters, or abusers. They often become pregnant or addicted as teenagers. This child provides the key to the family secrets. Nevertheless, this child is the most emotionally honest child in the family. They act out the tension and anger the other family members ignore. This child provides a distraction from the core issues in the family. The scapegoat usually has trouble in school because they get attention from negative behavior.

These children are usually the most sensitive and caring. They feel tremendous hurt and pain.

They are romantics who become very cynical and distrustful. They have a lot of self-hatred and self-destructive behavior.

In our family, Herman has traditionally taken this role. Even as a young child, he began acting out. Earline was in elementary school. During recess, her class went out to the playground. As Earline looked through the fence, there was Herman on his bicycle. He was probably two years old. The teacher refused to let her take him home. We lived near the school. Herman had slipped off and I didn't know where to find him. That was twenty-one years ago. He can still remember the tears in his sister's eyes as she looked at him through the fence. Today, he still slips off.

When he was around five years old, he was supposed to be outside, playing in the yard. When it started getting dark, I missed him. Earline and I walked through the nearby trailers calling his name. He didn't respond. We questioned all of his friends. No one knew what had happened to him. We were forced to call the police. The officer walked around the trailers shining his flashlight beneath them. Herman was found beneath one of them. He was asleep.

When we moved into a house, he developed

another trick. He took one of my lawn chairs and placed it at the edge of the fence in the backyard. He placed another chair on the opposite side of the fence. This was to help him make a speedy escape when he jumped the fence. To correct this problem, I added barbwire to the fence. This didn't stop him.

"Placater" - "Mascot"

This child takes responsibility for the emotional well-being of the family. They become the family's "social director" and clown, diverting the family's attention from the pain and anger. This child fills in for the absent or addicted parent. This role can overlap with the "Hero" in the family. This is one of the roles that I took on as an adult in our family. This child learns to rely on their charming personality. As adults they may rely on their personality rather than their intellect or skills to survive in life. This may prevent them from learning many important life lessons because they are able to take shortcuts.

This was often Herman's role in the family. He's a real charmer. Although he acts out the dysfunction in the family, he is also warm and affectionate. Herman is a very giving and compassionate friend. He prefers to discuss only the positive that he sees in people.

A number of years ago, Herman enrolled in college. He was seventeen. A lady working at the college knew both of us. When she saw us on campus, she gave Herman a warning.

Smiling, she said, "I'm going to be watching you."

With a sly look in his eyes, he said, "I'll be

watching you, too!"

The lady was in her late fifties or early sixties. When Mama found out about this, she told Herman that she didn't approve of him flirting with someone her age. Herman laughed. He has the potential to make any woman feel as if she is special. Even as a child, adults often told him their problems.

The Placater's whole self-definition is centered on others. Yet, they lack the ability to get their needs met. This child becomes an adult who is valued for their kind heart, generosity, and ability to listen to others. They become adults who cannot receive love, only give it. They often get involved in abusive relationships in an attempt to "save" the other person. They go into the helping professions

and become counselors, nurses, social workers, and therapists. They have very low self-worth and a lot of guilt

.

"Responsible Child" - "Family Hero"

This is the child who is "7 going on 50." This child takes over the parent's role at a very young age. They become very responsible and self-sufficient. They give the family self-worth because they look good on the outside. They are the good students, the sports stars, the prom queens. They may also be the Christian in the family or the moral person in the family. They may also be the drug dealers who have the most money in the family. They usually carry a lot of weight in the family. As adults, other family members may seek their counsel or financial assistance in times of crisis.

The parents look to this child to prove that they are good parents and good people. Siblings may develop this same respect. Their opinions are usually valued. What happens when they give bad advice to family members? Because this appears the only successful person in the family, others may take their bad advice rather than accept this person as fallible.

As an adult, the "Responsible Child" may meddle in the relationship of their siblings. They may suffer from a false belief that they know what's best for the other members of the family. This was one of the problems in my relationship with Henry. The "Responsible Child" was unable to identify appropriate boundaries.

Earline usually took this role in our family.

She was a good student. Academically, she achieved many accomplishments. Her success allowed me to pretend that I was a good parent. As a child, she often assisted with caring for her brother. She was often very vocal about how problems with Herman should be handled. As a young adult, she even attended several of Herman's school conferences, while I was at work. If the school needed a parent to pick Herman up from school immediately, she was willing to serve in this role. Actually, I grew tired of the school calling me about his behavior.

Earline didn't think that I knew how to handle Herman. As his older sibling, she had assisted with his childcare and began to view herself as a second mother responsible for his welfare. Eventually, she got her own chance to handle him. When he was sixteen, he enrolled in a college in Atlanta. Earline was attending law school at Georgia State University. However, she was living in Athens, Georgia. Herman moved in with her. She quickly learned that she didn't have the answers either. On more than one occasion, he disappeared on her.

It seemed that every night I was on the telephone with her trying to talk her through an emergency. He seldom showed up on time to meet her. He missed the train. He went to sleep on the train and passed his stop. He decided to go visit one of his cousins in Atlanta. Eventually, I packed him up and brought him home. Maybe packed is not the right word. I knew he was prone to slip off so I picked him up and drove back to Columbus. I told him that we would get his belongings later.

As an adult, the "Family Hero" is rigid, controlling, and extremely judgmental of others and privately of themselves. They achieve "success" on the outside and get lots of positive attention. However, they are cut off from their inner emotional life. They are compulsive and driven as adults because deep inside they feel inadequate and insecure.

And shall not God avenge His own
elect, which cry day and night
unto Him, though He bear
long with them?
Luke 18:7

The members of a family may change roles at times or have characteristics of more than one role. What happens when the scapegoat becomes successful? It upsets the family dynamics. Although the family is dysfunctional, they function as a family. When the scapegoat changes, it forces everyone else to reevaluate their own behavior. This change signals that everybody can do better. This change is often unacceptable to the family. Subconsciously, they may seek to put the scapegoat back in place. A vulnerable person will negate their success in an effort to continue as part of the family. It takes courage and commitment to break away from the family's dysfunction.

What happens when the "Hero" does something unacceptable? The family may excuse, ignore, minimize, or justify the behavior. If this family member decides to abandon their role completely, the family may assist them in returning to their original path.

When Earline decided that she wasn't going off to college, this was unacceptable to me. She said that she would attend a local college. For years, I had planned on her attending college outside of Columbus. For most of her life, she had expressed a desire to be a lawyer. There were no local law schools.

I had plans for Earline. She was going to accomplish the things that I had failed to do. I began to encourage her that she could do anything. There was no excuse for settling for less. In the process of encouraging her, I realized there was no excuse for me. My encouragement to her convicted me. If it was so simple, why couldn't I do it? In order for me to convince Earline, I had to take the first step. Taking my own advice, I enrolled in college. Earline followed suit and enrolled in the University of Georgia. She obtained three degrees. She has a bachelor in Sociology and one in Religion. She has a Masters in Social Work. She has also attended law school at Georgia State University.

So if you break the smallest
commandment and teach others to
do the same, you will be the least in
the Kingdom of Heaven. But anyone
who obeys God's laws and
teaches them will be great
in the Kingdom of Heaven.
Matthew 5:19 NLT

Dysfunctional families cause lots of harm. They cause lots of offenses. What do you do when a person who meant no harm causes you harm? What do you do when a person who meant no offense causes you offense? Receive no harm. Take no offense. Stand on the Word of God and receive the salvation of God. Pray for the person who has caused you harm. Pray for the person who has caused you offense. Pray twice as hard for the person who taught them how to cause offense or harm.

Headship Clarified

Therefore, anyone who becomes as humble as this little child is the greatest in the Kingdom of Heaven.
Matthew 18:4 NLT

When Henry and I reconciled our marriage for the third time, we started out right. It appeared that he was ready to lead the family. Our first day together was a day of continuous prayer. Henry initiated the prayers. We made a long list of promises to protect our marriage. We would study our Bibles together. We wouldn't go to bed angry. And so the list continued.

1. Headship is not dictatorship. The Bible does not give the husband permission to set up a dictatorship in the home. Husbands are not to lord their authority over their family but exercise it in humility.

"For the husband is the head of the wife, as Christ also is the head of the church, He Himself being the Savior of the body." Christ is not the dictator but the lover and

Savior of the church.
Ephesians 5:23

2. Headship does not mean that the husband is superior. Men and women have an equal standing before Christ.

There is neither Jew nor Greek, there is neither bond nor free, there is neither male nor female: for ye are all one in Christ Jesus.
Galatians 3:28

3. Headship does not mean that the husband must make all the decisions for the household. Husbands are told to manage their households. A wise manager does not make decisions in areas of incompetence. He delegates authority.

Let the deacons be the husbands of one wife, ruling their children and their own houses well.
I Timothy 3:12

4. Headship does not mean that the husband is always right. It does mean that he is responsible for the decisions that are made.

5. Headship is not to be demanded. Husbands are commanded to love their wives, not to make them submit by lecturing and haranguing them.

The husband's God-given task is nothing less than a leadership of love:

In the same way husbands ought to love their wives as their own bodies.
Ephesians 5: 28

There could be no higher analogy of a husband's love for his wife. It is to be modeled after Christ's supreme passion for the church. This love is rooted in self-sacrifice. Like Christ, husbands are told to give themselves up for the spiritual welfare of their wives. They are called to protect their wives physically, emotionally, and spiritually. The husband is to be the initiator not only in leadership but also in love.

As the husband puts the wife first, he pours love into her. He has to put her needs first. Until a man learns to do this, his desires will be selfish. God gave Adam Eve to help him avoid becoming selfish. All sin is born out of selfishness. As he nourishes her, she will pour love back into him.

The Hebrew meaning of the phrase "help meet" in the Word of God is simply "one who helps." The Bible teaches that it is the wife's duty to HELP her husband. There is no greater role for a woman in this world than being at her husband's side. A husband and wife are to be a team but someone's got to be in charge or else there is going be a house divided, a two-headed monster.

The old sinful nature loves to do evil,

which is just opposite from
what the Holy Spirit wants.
Galatians 5:17

The Bible teaches that it is God's will for women to get married, have children, and manage their household. God is saying that a woman should work at home. "Managing the house," means that she is to take care of the business of the home. Being a full-time mother or housewife is a tremendous amount of work! We live in a time when most women also work outside of the home.

What happens when economics prevent the wife from staying at home? What happens when the wife is forced by circumstances to work outside the home? What happens when the job outside the home is just as taxing as the job in the home?

Husbands need to love their wives as God commands. Wives need to obey their husbands as it is right in the Lord. A wife would be much more likely to submit if her husband would start to be fair and show her more respect and love. The Bible is clear; a wife is commanded to be in subjection to her **own** husband.

Unrealistic expectations or desires will kill any relationship. We live in a society and a culture that does a poor job of portraying healthy, realistic expectations for a relationship. There are needs that God wants us to meet for our partner, that He will equip us to meet. There are other needs that only God can meet. We cannot expect any person to meet the needs that God wants to meet for us. We must realize our limitations and not step outside of our God-given roles.

The stereotypical American household of the 1950s, depicted in innumerable television comedies, was built around an awkward, well-meaning, indulgent father continually confused by his intelligent and more manipulating wife and children. Today other images of fathers are portrayed, and men must experience public heat of a different kind. A once bumbling father has become a savage, the perpetrator of injustice in the home, an abuser of children and women who are helpless, weak, and enslaved in marriage. Although incidences of domestic violence committed by men are at an all-time high, men don't perpetrate all violent acts. Women also abuse.

There was a time when American wives praised their husbands by calling them "good providers." Sarah called Abraham "Lord." The ordinary working man was praised for his ability to maintain a wife and children without assistance. These days appear to be gone forever.

Being a good provider often required a man to commit himself early to a career and to stay in it until his retirement. This had very little to do with whether or not he enjoyed the work or was suited for it. Men were also moved to scream, "Is there more to life than this?" The imagination often answered this question. Our imagination can work for good or evil. Our imagination can also play tricks on us.

A man's pride shall bring him low:
but honour shall uphold

the humble in spirit.
Proverbs 29:23

Whenever partners have incompatible methods of resolving conflict, the issues may never truly be resolved. Pride can hinder any relationship. Each spouse should strengthen the other spouse. Where one spouse is weak, the other should be strong. The wife's duty and responsibility is to be a *helpmeet* for her husband. God provides through the wife the things that the husband needs to become successful.

If the husband's pride hinders him from accepting the help that God has provided him through his wife, it hinders his potential for growth. Inadvertently, he sets himself up for failure. If the husband requests help and the wife doesn't freely provide it, she moves outside her God-given role. By destroying the order of the family, she sets the family up for failure.

For God is not a God of
disorder but of peace.
1 Corinthians 14:33 NLT

When Henry and I separated, this further disturbed the order of our home. The effects were immediately felt. I wanted to believe that I could compensate for his absence. Things are in danger of remaining out of order whenever God's will is not the primary consideration in any relationship. This is even more crucial in marriage. Any argument ends when we look into the word of God for honest answers and are willing to obey the instructions or corrections found therein.

God is our refuge and strength, a
very present help in trouble.
Therefore will not we fear, though
the earth be removed, and though
the mountains be carried into the
midst of the sea; though the waters
thereof roar and be troubled,
though the mountains shake
with the swelling thereof.
Psalm 46:1-3

It is crucial in any household for the spouses to wholeheartedly submit to God. When this doesn't occur, God's order for the home is violated. God desires that the husband be the spiritual and economic head of the house. The woman is to be his helper or assistant. She is to assist him in maintaining the order of house. In order for the husband to establish and retain order, he must maintain a consistent channel of communication with the Lord.

A godly wife will find comfort in submitting to her husband when she trusts him to fulfill his role as the head of the family. In any marriage, God's grace is able to sustain the marriage. When the spouses do not totally submit to the will of God, order is not established in the family. It is only God's grace that holds any marriage relationship together.

Keep me from deliberate sins! Don't let them control me. Then I will be free of guilt and innocent of great sin.
Psalm 19:13

Our household was left out of order, when Henry decided not to consult God about the future of our relationship. This was his free choice to make. The husband is responsible for his wife. The wife is not responsible for her husband or his choices. When I realized that things were out of order, I began to seek God for the answer. During my obsession with my marital problems, my communication with Him had been broken. When God began to deal with me, He showed me the error of my ways.

If we confess our sins to Him, He is faithful and just to forgive us.
1 John 1:9 NLT

For my part in the chaos, I needed to repent. Not only did I need to repent to God, I needed to repent to Henry. Without hesitation, I did both. Since Henry was avoiding me, I sent him a balloon bouquet to his job. He didn't respond. That's not my concern. **I did what God required of me.**

The Ain'ts Have it

Regard not them that have familiar spirits, neither seek after wizards, to be defiled by them: I am the LORD your God.
Leviticus 19:31

Many people assume that those who call themselves by the name Christians or saints are representatives of Christ. Christian means "Christ-like." When those who profess the name of Christ manifest behaviors that are inconsistent with the nature of Christ, they cause sinners to blaspheme the name of God. By their very behavior, they suggest this is the way Christ would act in this situation.

What has happened to the teachings of the aged women? Do we wink at sin? Do we excuse sin for convenience sake? At what cost are we willing to ignore sin? How can darkness be excused as light? Is there still a difference between clean and unclean? Is there a difference between holy and unholy? What fellowship does light have with darkness?

There are times when I am asked to provide advice for someone who is struggling with some issue. In many of these instances, I am keenly aware that I only have one version of the problem to work with. Unless I have all the facts, I listen. If after verbalizing their problems, they are still seeking an answer, I point them to the Word of God.

In a marriage crisis, I am careful not to assume ownership of their problems or give them biased advice. Not every good idea is a God idea. I'm ever mindful that what God has put together, I have no right to separate.

For those seeking advice, let me offer a word of warning.

- Be sure to seek Godly counsel
- Consider the advisor's history in this area, i.e., do they have unresolved issues in this area
- Consider the person's lifestyle? What have they accomplished by taking their own advice?
- Does the Word support the advice?
- Never take advice from someone who has nothing to lose, when you have everything to lose.
- Are there hidden motives?
- Is this person someone who has a proven history of standing with you through difficult times? A wrong decision may have lasting negative consequences.

The person who is a second spouse may choose to stand on the teachings of the Old Testament, which strictly forbade a husband remarrying his first wife after either of them had been remarried. What is difficult for some to understand is that the divorce is real. It breaks the original covenant. A divorce is sinful when it occurs for any reason other than those identified in the scriptures. However, although sinful, the second marriage covenant is real. Nonetheless, once married, a person is truly married. The covenant is made, the bonds to the first marriage are untied, and the bonds to the second marriage are firmly knotted.

As a true marriage, though improperly made, sex within the bounds of a remarriage is sanctified by that marriage contract. Healthy sexual relations inside a remarriage are nowhere called sins. To the person who takes this stand, I say be careful of becoming legalistic.

When a man hath taken a wife, and married her, and it come to pass that she find no favour in his eyes, because he hath found some uncleanness in her: then let him write her a bill of divorcement, and give it in her hand, and send her out of his house. And when she is departed out of his house, she may go and be another man's wife. And if the latter husband hate her, and write her a bill of divorcement, and giveth it in her hand, and sendeth her out of his house; or if the latter husband die, which took her to be his wife; Her former husband, which sent her

away, may not take her again to be his wife, after that she is defiled; for that is abomination before the Lord: and thou shalt not cause the land to sin, which the Lord thy God giveth thee for an inheritance.
Deuteronomy 24:1-4

A person with a liberal view of marriage may use divorce as a way to avoid an adulterous relationship. Their excuse may be God has called us to peace. My advice to this person, Jesus is still the Prince of Peace. No relationship without Him as the foundation will ever have peace.

Thou hast walked in the way of thy sister; therefore will I give her cup into thine hand. Thus saith the Lord GOD; Thou shalt drink of thy sister's cup deep and large: thou shalt be laughed to scorn and had in derision; it containeth much. Thou shalt be filled with drunkenness and sorrow, with the cup of astonishment and desolation, with the cup of thy sister Samaria.
Ezekiel 23:31-33

The third person to avoid taking advice from

is a wounded first spouse. This person may have a desire to reconcile with their former spouse. If this is not a viable option, they may have difficulty accepting this fact. Their advice may be based on what they would like to see happen in their own life. This person may inadvertently encourage destroying a second family. To this person, I say, seek God for deliverance or resolutions for your own situation.

But let none of you suffer as a murderer, or as a thief, or as an evildoer, or as a busybody in other men's matters.
1 Peter 4:15

Any person who has been single too long has the potential to give dangerous advice. They are prone to be busybodies. A person who has an extremely negative experience in marriage will give advice based on previous experiences.

Over the years, I have received lots of unsolicited advice about my relationship with Henry. Although well meaning, much of it found no basis or application in the scriptures. I have received emails, heard messages, and telephone calls that say some people just can't go where you are going. That may be true. One person has told me for years to 'forget him because he's simply not worth the trouble.' This person has an extremely poor track record. Finally, to that person I said, "I'm not going to do that."

The LORD doesn't make decisions the way you do! People judge by outward appearance but the LORD looks at a person's thoughts and intentions.
1 Samuel 16:7 NLT

A number of years ago, I met a lady who had known my husband since his childhood. She was shocked to discover who my husband was.

After being introduced to me, she said. "You're married to who? And you work where? And you have been to college? And you have how many degrees? And you are married to a jailbird! You are a fool! He is good looking and nice but he's a jail-bird. You have to be a fool! You are a smart fool but a fool!"

Last week, I saw her again and she asked me how he was doing. When I told her we were separated, she got me again.

"You mean that you are really separated! Is he on something? Well, it's your fault. I told you when I met you to leave that jailbird alone! You had him looking good too... That' all I have to say. You asked for that! Don't you ever dress a man up!"

"For the lips of a priest ought to preserve knowledge, and from his

mouth men should seek instruction - because he is the messenger of the Lord Almighty. But you have turned from the way and by your teaching have caused many to stumble..."
Malachi 2: 7-8 NIV

The last people that I'm going to address in this section are the false prophets. A true prophet is known by the accuracy of his prophecies. They aren't half-truths. The prophecies aren't based on prior knowledge of the situation. To you, I say seek to discover your spiritual gifts. God will never use you in the gift of prophecy until you learn to retain knowledge.

"Beware of false prophets who come disguised as harmless sheep but are really wolves that will tear you apart.
Matthew 7:15 NLT

I have been blessed with a friend who can give me godly counsel. During this difficult time, Esther has coached me through. She didn't side with me or with Henry. On the days when I was overly obsessed with the problems, she encouraged me to stay focused.

Repeatedly, she said, "Come on Charlotte. Stay focused. You have too much to do. It's not about you. It's not about Buck. This has come to get you sidetracked. Pull out your computer and get started on the next book. You have to stay in that place with God. Don't let this pull you out of place."

Divorce is clearly a sin against God and the sacred covenant of marriage but it is not an unforgivable sin. The instant a divorced person says, "I do" to a new marriage covenant with a new spouse, they have "altered" their first marriage contract. They have changed its terms, disregarded its legality, and torn away the rope that bound that relationship. At that instant, they have made the previous contract null, void, and irreparable.

'I hate divorce,' says the Lord God of Israel, "... So guard yourself in your spirit, and do not break faith. You have wearied the Lord with your words. 'How have we wearied Him?' you ask. By saying, 'All who do evil are good in the eyes of the Lord, and He is pleased with them' or 'Where is the God of justice?'"

Malachi 2: 13-17 NIV

When it came to the problems in my marriage with Henry, there was plenty of blame to go around. We could blame the problems on the drugs or on the lifestyle. However, we made the choice to indulge in both. We could blame our problems on those who sowed the seeds of discord in our relationship. While God will not hold them blameless, we made the choice to entertain them. Our history was strong and deep. We had weathered too many storms together. No one should have been able to persuade either of us to destroy the other. Yet, when we allowed a crack in our foundation, we opened the door of destruction for our marriage.

Blessed are the peacemakers:
for they shall be called
the children of God.
Matthew 5:9

In the midst of this confusion, my question is where were the peacemakers? It was no secret that Henry and I were having problems. It's sad to say that not one person offered to pray with us or counsel us. Why was it that no one tried to help or intercede? There are many possible reasons, a lack of compassion, inconvenience, or being consumed by their own problems. Perhaps, they were just tired of the drama between Henry and me. Perhaps, they assumed that we would work our differences out as in times past. Would we have listened? Would it have helped? Honestly, I don't know. Although the problems stemmed from minor disagreements, we had magnified them.

He that turneth away his ear from
hearing the law, even his prayer
shall be abomination.
Proverbs 28:9

It is even sadder that many professing Saints sided with one of us. Some professing Saints took it a step further. They attempted to justify Henry's actions, insisting that he was growing closer to the Lord. He was reported to be praying, reading his Bible, and obeying the Word. They insisted the Lord was blessing him while he was openly living in adultery. I was told these same things when Henry was involved with Sister Juanita. One person insisted that they were both saved. When I asked about Henry spending the night at Sister Juanita's apartment, their actions were excused. She stated, "He must be sleeping in a chair. I know they are both saved."

No wonder judgment is going to begin at the house of God. It is professing Christians who have done the most to hurt the cause of Christ. Some people who lack this same confession have principles, morals, and ethics that are stronger than many professing Christians do.

Henry was encouraged to get his life in order by committing a second sin of divorcing a faithful spouse to marry his mistress. Henry said he was in the will of God. When did God's will ever deviate from His Word? For Henry it happened when he was assured of this by someone he respected. At least, this is how he justified his actions.

On a number of occasions, I was told, "I can't believe we are in the same place that we were last year." Although I didn't comment, I couldn't believe it either. The same person who had encouraged his relationship with Sister Juanita also encouraged his relationship with Varetta.

There was no right or wrong side between Henry and me. The Word of God is always right. Sin breeds sin. Openly practicing sin clouds our ability to judge right from wrong and good from evil. What good is salt when it has lost its savor?

For the name of God is
blasphemed among the Gentiles
through you, as it is written.
Romans 2:24

Most professing Christians need to become Christians. It is more difficult to get professing Christians to become Christians than non- Christians. It is time for a return to transformational conversions.

Dear children, continue to live in
fellowship with Christ so that when
He returns, you will be full of
courage and not shrink
back from Him in shame.
1 John 2:28 NLT

Henry and I were both at fault and we knew it. However, we were both trying to teach each other a lesson. The referees were biased and self-serving. This situation has brought shame not only to us, our families, those who took part in the deception but also to the body of Christ. In the end, we both lost the game.

A Dying Divorce

How precious is Your unfailing love, O God! All humanity finds shelter in the shadow of Your wings.
Psalm 36:7 NLT

In many ways a divorce is a death. It marks the death of a relationship, a commitment, a covenant, and sometimes a family. As such, it carries all the emotions associated with any loss. It is important to allow the grieving process to complete before moving on to a new relationship. The healing takes time. Many experts estimate that it takes one year of healing for every five years of the relationship.

In any disagreement or difference of opinions, it is vital to good communication to remain agreeable to an amicable resolution. This is doubly important when considering a divorce. When the feuding parties are more interested in winning the conflict than reaching a positive resolution, healthy communication does not occur. Indeed, sometimes the conflict turns deadly.

Most experts list four basic stages of recovery for divorce:

- Survival: There are more responsibilities but less

income: more demands but less energy. The pace is often frantic and filled with the anxieties of learning to cope alone. One person must now repair the car, balance the checkbook, do the laundry and prepare the meals.

- Grief: A precious relationship has died and divorced people must grieve. We can't sleep. We lose weight. It is often difficult to concentrate. There are too many memories. An old song on the radio often brings tears.
- Identity: This is also known as the crazy stage. It could be as subtle as redecorating the house to buying a new car, changing jobs, moving to a new city, going back to school or quickly getting involved in a new relationship. It can be an exciting but dangerous time of discovery.
- Directions: We are becoming more comfortable with who we are as single adults. We begin to think about our future. We are going to survive. Eventually, we will find wholeness.

Thou wilt keep him in perfect peace,
whose mind is stayed on Thee:
because he trusteth in Thee.
Isaiah 26:3

Each of these stages takes time to complete. It is important for us to be patient with others and ourselves. It is a time to grow closer to God. It's a time for redirection and fellowship. This can also be a time of reflection and personal growth.

Before Henry and I separated, I began to feel

numerous emotions, distrust, unappreciated, used, violated, stressed, and frustrated. More than that, I felt something dying inside of me. This was an emotion that I had never felt before. The other emotions were familiar to me. The feelings of grief were new.

Henry has been a part of my life for a long time. There were times that I believed I would never survive without him. There were times that I was just as obsessed with him as he was with that car. There were times when my life centered around his needs and his prison sentences. There were times when I neglected my safety and security because of my relationship with him. There were times when I took responsibility for his recovery. All of that was changing. I thought my feelings for him were dying. It was actually co-dependency dying. My need for him was dying. It was replaced with a desire. I wish to do the perfect will of my Heavenly Father. In the area of marriage, I had failed miserably.

In the recent months, I have experienced another set of emotions, denial, bargaining, shock, elation, and depression. Rather than setting things in order and allowing peace to return to the home, the separation further disturbed the order of the home. It affected everything in my life. It clouded my vision and perception of reality. There were days when I was excited and appeared to be thriving again. Out of nowhere, the tears would come. Sadness would come. For no explainable reason, grief would set in again.

For this cause shall a man leave his
father and mother, and shall be

joined unto his wife, and they two shall be one flesh.
Ephesians 5:31

As in times past, I had been knocked down. The very core of my being had been shaken. We were going through a very difficult situation, yet the bond was still intact. We both wanted it severed but it wasn't something that we created. God created the bond. Henry chose to deal with his pain by attempting to stay angry with me and moving on with an ungodly relationship.

Therefore I was left alone, and saw this great vision, and there remained no strength in me: for my comeliness was turned in me into corruption, and I retained no strength. Yet heard I the voice of His words: and when I heard the voice of His words, then was I in a deep sleep on my face, and my face toward the ground. And, behold, an hand touched me, which set me upon my knees and upon the palms of my hands.
Daniel 10:8-10

I chose to do what I've done before. I fell on my face. I cried out to the God of my Salvation. I cried out to the one who has promised me a hope and a future. I cried out to my Redeemer. I cried out to the Living God. I cried out to the Bread of Heaven. I cried out to my Provider. I cried out to the God that heals me. I cried out to the Everlasting God. I cried out to the Prince of Peace.

After acknowledging who He is in my life, I acknowledged the wrong that I had done. I asked Him to forgive me for my shortcomings. I asked Him to forgive me for handling things my way. I asked Him to forgive me for the problems in the marriage. I asked Him to forgive me for not being more forgiving.

When I had finished asking for forgiveness for my sins, I prayed for Henry. I asked God to restore him in mercy. I asked God to remove the scales from his eyes. I asked God to renew his mind. I asked God to repair the damage that the drugs had caused.

Hatred stirs up quarrels but
love covers all offenses.
Proverbs 10:12 NLT

When I finished praying for Henry, I prayed for those who aided the deception. I prayed for their salvation. I prayed for Varetta's salvation. I prayed for God to forgive everybody that had been involved in the treacherous scheme.

After praying for them, I asked God to restore order to my life. I asked Him to restore everything that the devil had stolen from me. I prayed for the joy of my salvation to be restored.

When I finished praying for restoration, I asked for direction. I asked God to order my footsteps. I asked Him to lead me and guide me in the knowledge of the truth. I asked Him to bring glory to His name in the midst of this situation.

When I was assured that God had not only heard me but had answered me, I arose from the floor. My strength had returned. Assured that God was on my side, I was prepared to go on. I had been weak but God had made me strong.

And whatsoever ye do, do it heartily,
as to the Lord, and not unto men;
Knowing that of the Lord ye shall
receive the reward of the
inheritance: for ye serve
the Lord Christ.
Colossians 3:23-24

I know who I am. I know whose I am. I am fully persuaded that nothing by any means shall separate me from the love of God. I am committed to run this race to the finish. I'll wait patiently on the manifestation of God. I'll complete the purpose that God has for my life.

I'm no longer taking responsibility for Henry. His salvation is between him and God. His drug addiction is between him and God. Nothing is going to stand between God and me. That includes my love for Henry Johnson.

A Dream Deferred

We who have fled to Him for refuge can take new courage, for we can hold on to His promise with confidence.
Hebrews 6:18-19

There is increasing doubt that God really can change lives. Many doubt the value of a "crisis conversion" in bringing meaningful deliverance. Can God deliver people from drug addiction? In a moment! Can He repair a marriage? In an instant! Can God deliver a homosexual? Can He repair drug-induced brain damage? Free anyone from lust? Surely, He can!

Over sixteen years ago, God told me to tell the whole story because this was an opportunity to glorify Him. My limited understanding didn't comprehend the magnitude of what He meant. Over the years, He has made His instructions increasingly clearer to me. This was the birth of Reaching Beyond the Breaks Ministries. Henry has always been a part of my vision for my ministry. Now, it appears that my dream has been altered or deferred. Delay does not mean denial. Should my dream cease because Henry is out of place? I think not!

You will keep on guiding me
with Your counsel, leading

me to a glorious destiny.
Psalm 73:24 NLT

Since I surrendered my life to Christ, there has always been the assuring knowledge that He was going to use my life for His glory. Although there have been times when I strayed from the path of righteousness, this assurance in my heart never dissipated. God has called me to evangelism. My passion is to see souls saved, to see lives changed.

An evangelist is a messenger charged to deliver an urgent message. Many things can be said about a messenger but what matters most is the message. The word we bring is the greatest news ever spoken or heard. Evangelists are people with a passion to know the living God, the Son, and the Holy Spirit. They are charged to make His grace and love known to every person on earth.

My soul is also sore vexed:
but Thou, O LORD, how long?
Psalm 6:3

We have to step out of the boat. Faith is risking before we see results. It wasn't Peter who failed when he stepped out of the boat and began to sink. It was the eleven who waited to see what would happen to Peter.

He has not punished us for all our
sins, nor does He deal with us, as we
deserve. For His unfailing love to-

wards those who fear Him is as
great as the heights of the heavens
above the earth. He removed our
rebellious acts as far as the east
from the west.
Psalm 104:10-12 NLT

Great people are not used to perform the work of God but ordinary people who are committed to Him. Believers may say to God, "I am nothing. I have no gifts. I often fail miserably. Do You really want to use me?" The answer to that question is found in God's Word. He used the hesitant, inarticulate Moses to lead Israel to freedom (Exodus.3:13; 4:10). He used shepherds, as well as fishermen and farmers to accomplish His work and record His words. A simple carpenter and a peasant girl raised His Only Begotten Son.

God asked Abraham to give up Isaac so that He could make him the father of many nations. Whenever we deny ourselves something for Christ, He replaces it with something better. Whenever our hands are clutched ina fist, nothing goes out of it, and nothing can come into it. We have to open our hands to allow the distractions to be released from our life. Our hands will be left open to receive something more attractive. Sometimes, we hinder the purpose of God by trying to hold on to things or people that are distracting us from our purpose. Oh that I might know Him! I'm counting everything else as dung, waste.

Listen to my voice in the morning, LORD. Each morning I bring my requests to You and wait expectantly.
Psalm 5:3

Once, I allowed God to deal with the hurt in my heart, I was able to focus. I was able to see clearly. Even with Henry out of place, I stepped back into my place. My house and ministry began to come to order.

If Henry stays out of order, my dream will just be revised. There are many things Henry and I planned to do together. I'll still accomplish them. Although he has hurt me deeply on more than one occasion, I have also gained a wealth of knowledge from my relationship with him. He inspires me to excel. My problems with him keep me on my knees. It's through these problems that God's Word has become alive in my life. There are many lessons that I have learned from my relationship with him. They will remain a part of my writings. For these things, I am thankful.

It is pleasant to see dreams come true but fools will not turn from evil to attain them.
Proverbs 13:19 NLT

Henry may never materially participate in the things that I will accomplish with my ministry. He will, however, get credit for his inspiration. Often times when a loved one dies, the families will set up memorials, scholarships, or trust funds in that person's name. This is a way of celebrating what that person has brought to our life. A divorce is very much like a death.

For your shame ye shall have double;
and for confusion they shall rejoice
in their portion: therefore in their
land they shall possess the double:
everlasting joy shall be unto them.
Isaiah 61:7

Rather than becoming angry or vindictive because of the things that have happened in our relationship, I am going to celebrate the relationship. As I accomplish the things that we planned to do together, many of them will be named in his honor. Rather than hiding in shame or embarrassment because of the condition of our marriage, I have decided to tell the truth and bring shame to those who would love to rejoice at my sufferings.

Wherefore be ye not unwise but un-
derstanding what the
will of the Lord is.
Ephesians 5:17

You see it's not about me. It's not about Henry. It's about a God who still desires holiness. It's about God who still puts a difference between clean and unclean. It's about a God who looks beyond our failures to see what we have the potential to become. Life is short and it's not about us. Eternity is long and it's all about God. He still hates divorce and He still hates sin. He still desires a relationship with His people.

Some things may seem hurtful but they are meant for our good. Once we have been healed we have a command, "when thou art converted strengthen thy brother." Somehow, we have missed this commandment. So many times rather than building up, we tear down. Rather than looking down to help others up, we look down to see if there is anybody beneath us if there is nobody there we find someone. If they're not far enough down, we push them lower. Why? When we look down on others, somehow knowing that we aren't on the bottom of the barrel makes us feel better about ourselves. WHY? In the shelter of our insecurities, we hide under the shadow of the failures of others. If only we could be real with God, and risk being made free.

I no longer count on my own goodness or my ability to obey God's law but I trust Christ to save me.
Philippians 3:9 NLT

Henry has been seeking to be free mentally for a long time. He hasn't quite found this freedom. He has found a substitute mother. One day, he will handle his own business and make his own decisions. Prayerfully, the first decision he will make will be to ask God for direction. In my efforts to aid him in his quest for freedom, I have made many mistakes. These mistakes were not deliberate, meant to hurt him, or premeditated. This is not an attempt to excuse my sins.

My pregnancy is in the ninth month, and I'm about to give birth to the dreams and visions that God has given me. There are times when excitement borders on anxiousness and even tries to cross over to fear. However, I realize that I am walking in the will of God, and though the vision tarries, I'll wait. It shall surely come to pass.

Although the dream is deferred, it doesn't mean it won't come to pass. My actions and my failure to see the vision clearly delayed the dream. Although I'm doing my best, I realize that God gets the glory for this victory. In all my ways I am acknowledging Him. I am no longer leaning to my own understanding. I'm praying daily for God to order my steps in His Word, and to make my path plain and straight that I may not veer to the right or to the left. Whether through prayer, financial support or volunteerism, opportunities for helping to reach the world for Christ have never been more varied.

Rejoice evermore, Pray without ceasing. In everything give thanks: For this is the will of God in Christ Jesus Concerning you...Quench not the Spirit...Despise not

Prophesyings...Prove all things; Hold fast that which is good...Abstain from all Appearance of evil.
1 Thessalonians 5:16-22

To "Rejoice evermore" means to rejoice constantly, not only when things are going well but also when things aren't going well. To **"Pray without ceasing**" denotes a constant, unbreakable communion with God. We don't have to pray aloud. Our lips don't have to move. However, within our souls, there must be that continuing, ceaseless communion with our Heavenly Father.

"In everything give thanks" does not mean we give thanks for all things but rather IN ALL THINGS. Sometimes things don't go the way that we expect but we must continue to thank God for the GOOD THINGS HE HAS DONE.

It Doesn't Really Matter

"And if it seem evil unto you to serve the LORD, choose you this day whom ye will serve; whether the gods which your fathers served that were on the other side of the flood, or the gods of the Amorites, in whose land ye dwell: but as for me and my house, we will serve the LORD."

Joshua 24:15

When I was writing *A Journey to Hell and Back*, I had to come to place called *It Doesn't Matter*. Now, I find myself in that place again. When I came to the acceptance of writing that book, it was only after an agonizing process. There were countless tears and endless questions. Many of the questions had no answers. Some questions remain unanswered.

There are times when it seems all of that happened so long ago. There are other times when the pain seems like yesterday. When I meet people who are insensitive, there are times that I wish that I could take the book back. These thoughts are fleeting thoughts. In my heart, I know God has ordained the current path of my life.

As I was writing the first book, I thought about how my life would change after the book's release. To be honest, most of my thoughts were negative and selfish. I wondered how people would view me. I wondered if I would be able to find another job. I wondered if people would be hurt by my words. It never occurred to me that anything positive would come from revealing not just the source of my strength but also the source of my pain.

During one phase of my Aunt Bobbie and Earline's relationship, my aunt developed a favorite saying. She repeated this answer to everything said to her.

"It don't matter!"

This was a source of irritation for Earline. She hated this worse than being called F. Lee Bailey. One day Aunt Bobbie asked Earline a question.

"What's wrong with you, Earline?"

"It don't matter! It don't matter! It don't matter! That's all you know, 'It don't matter.'"

This was the place that I had to find as I was writing *A Journey to Hell and Back*. My sole purpose and desire had to become fulfilling the purpose and plan of God for my life. What others would say had to become insignificant. My personal comforts and discomforts had to be pushed aside. This wasn't easy. Truthfully, it was a very painful process. I had to become open and vulnerable.

And let us not be weary in well doing: for in due season we shall reap if we faint not.
Galatians 6:9

In my previous books, I chose to stray away

from the shady circumstances of my first marriage. The poem for this book was written almost a year ago. When I wrote the poem, I knew it was for my next book. However, I had no idea what the book would be about. When I realized what the subject matter would be, I wasn't sure that I could write this one. Many of the things written in this book were originally embarrassing to me. Before beginning the writing process, I pondered in my heart how I would discuss certain issues without seeming vindictive. The situation itself seems so ridiculous and unfathomable that I couldn't imagine how I could explain it.

When thou passest through the waters, I will be with thee; and through the rivers, they shall not overflow thee: when thou walkest through the fire, thou shalt not be burned; neither shall the flame kindle upon thee.
Isaiah 43:2

During recent months, I have asked myself countless questions. Do I still believe God even when I can't believe what just happened? How did we get here? Where do we go from here? Where will this end? When will it really end? How can You get glory out of this one? Have the last twenty-two years been a lie? Do I love Henry? Have I ever loved him? Does he love me? Has he ever loved me? Did I dream this? If this is a nightmare, when will I wake up? Should I wash my hands of him? Is this really worth the effort? Have I missed You, God? Why did I become involved with him? Why has it been so hard for us to end this thing? What changed in our relationship? Who sowed the seeds of discord between us? Where were all these opinionated people when I was standing behind this man? Who gave them the authority to interfere in our marriage? How my God can we overcome this one? If I walk away now, will I find myself back in this relationship five years from now? God have my prayers been in vain?

When your faith is tested, your endurance has a chance to grow.
James 1:3 NLT

And yes, during this time, I have been so shocked, that I have questioned my very existence. God has my life and my ministry meant anything? How can I reach others when I have caused so much pain to those closest to me? Will I ever get this thing right? Has everything that I have believed been a lie? Have I wasted my life? I know that I wasted my life prior to my salvation but have I continued to waste my life? God, how can I continue to speak or write about grace? Who will listen? How is this going to affect my ministry?

But now it is come upon thee, and thou faintest; it toucheth thee, and thou art troubled. Is not this thy

*fear, thy confidence, thy hope, and
the uprightness of thy ways?
Remember, I pray thee, who ever
perished, being innocent? or where
were the righteous cut off?*
Job 4:5-7

After I asked all of these questions, many of them remained unanswered. There are no easy explanations. All I know for sure is that in recent weeks, I have encountered a number of people who are in the midst of something that I am currently **going through**. In the midst of my own pain and confusion, I have yet had to offer them hope.

In this midst of this, I am reminded of Job. I'm going to trust Him. And while I trust Him, I'll maintain my integrity. Not only have I been faithful to my husband but I have also been faithful to my God. No matter what it looks like, no matter how it comes out I'm going to trust Him. I'm going to remain faithful. I won't seek revenge or retribution. I won't move to the right or to the left without receiving instruction from My God. While I'm waiting for God to move, I won't fan the flames of my flesh. If Henry should choose to end our marriage by divorce, I'm free to remarry. I'm not looking for a man or a husband. Should God choose to send one, I'll accept him as a gift from God. I won't be afraid to move at God's direction.

In the meantime, I've found that place again, the place where it doesn't matter. It doesn't matter what others think. There are no easy solutions. It doesn't matter how it works out. Yes, I have a way that I would like for this story to end. But more than this, I want God's will to be done in my life.

Those things, which ye have both learned, and received, and heard, and seen in me, do: and the God of peace shall be with you.
Philippians 4:9

"God nothing matters more to me than You. I surrender completely my will to You. Be Thou glorified!"

Epilogue

All of you should be of one mind, full of sympathy toward each other, loving one another with tender hearts and humble minds.
1 Peter 3:8

Grace Under Fire concluded with the beginning of our third marriage. There was no fairy tale ending. In real life, there is no prince charming on a white horse who is able to sweep us off our feet. There is no 'happily ever after.' Marriage is a commitment before God and man. It is a legal and religious vow to join together to become one flesh. Its express purpose is that a man and woman join together forsaking all others until the conclusion of their earthly lives. Now we find ourselves a year later, another infidelity, and contemplating another divorce.

No individual in their own strength can overcome some of the difficulties that can arise in marriage. Only God's grace can sustain a marriage through these stressful situations. He's waiting to help.

When communication breaks down or ceases to exist, the injured parties may take refuge. They may find shelter in the wrong places or with the wrong people. When they decide the marriage is hopeless and there are no reasonable solutions to their differences, chaos may ensue.

Things are in danger of remaining out of order whenever God's will is not the primary consideration in any relationship. This is even more crucial in marriage. Any argument ends when we look into the word of God for honest answers and are willing to obey the instructions or corrections found therein.

God has a resolution for any conflict. It's found in His Word. When communication and actions move to a *tit-for-tat* mode, someone will always lose. In the end, both partners lose.

Today, there are many reasons why a marriage ends. It is not my intention to preach for or against divorce. There are enough teachings in this area. These teachings range from rigid to liberal. I'm not offering a moral judgment concerning divorce. It is my desire that neither marriage nor divorce be entered into lightly. It should not be considered as a transient state. Marriage is a commitment to pray for each other. It is a vow to love even when the love is not convenient and when all hope appears to be gone. A word of love can make a world of difference.

A ceremony and legal forms provide the legal commitment but only God can unite two people into one. Partners should complement each other. Each partner's strengths and weaknesses enter into this union. Spouses should be an asset to their partners.

It is better not to make a vow than to make one and break it. Entering into our third marriage, **I decided** that this time, I would work with him to fight to preserve this union and keep our family together. Once, we renewed our vows. Four times, we have promised before God, our family, and civil authorities that we would bear each other's infirmities, share our highs as well as our lows, and strengthen each other. We even promised to share our finances. Each time, it was our intention that our marriage would flourish and edify our family.

As in any abusive relationship, the honeymoon period would always be romantic and idyllic. Abuse comes in varying forms. Rather than focusing on working out the core issues in our marriage, we were swept up into the romance and the excitement of our relationship. We dreamed of the perfect union. We failed to find a balance between the war and the honeymoon. Sometimes, it appeared that we created the war to get to the honeymoon.

Years of turbulence and conflict enable us to amplify each other's weaknesses. It is easy to belittle and destroy each other and our marriage. It takes the Lord to overcome years of emotional abuse on both sides. It takes time and patience to locate and illuminate the strengths in our relationship. We must constantly ask the Lord to guide us and order our steps in His Word.

Give your burdens to the LORD, and
He will take care of you. He will not
permit the godly to slip and fall.
Psalm 55:22 NLT

The storms of life won't harm us if we have deep roots in God. During the difficult times, it is often convenient to think of separation or divorce. For us, separation has often been a temporary solution to our extreme communication problems. While arguing, it often feels that all love and hope is gone. While tempers are flaring, it seems that life apart is a desirable state. These are the times that God's grace is sufficient to sustain the weakest marriage.

Thou wilt shew me the path of life:
in Thy presence is fulness of joy; at
Thy right hand there are pleasures
for evermore.
Psalm 16:11

Following each of our divorces, the separation allowed us to reexamine the importance of our marriage and the importance of our relationship. Each time we divorced, the marriage was dissolved legally but not emotionally. The attachment between us was always clearer when we were separated. This time, outside manipulators have clouded the picture.

In order to sustain any marriage, we must pray without ceasing. The Lord is able to keep that which is committed unto Him. Often, we attempt to salvage a marriage but without God, it is pointless.

And we know that all things work to-
gether for good to them that love
God, to them who are the called ac-

cording to his purpose.
Romans 8:28

This time, we created more chaos and devastation. God already knows how this one will end. Time and patience will reveal His perfect will and plan for our lives. Rather than settling for a quick and seemingly easy solution, I've decided to let God have this battle.

Everyone will know that the LORD does not need weapons to rescue His people. It is His battle, not ours.
1 Samuel 17:47 NLT

My efforts have messed things up on more than one occasion. The first divorce lasted over five years. We have been separated more times than I can remember. In spite of all the drama, hurt, and embarrassment, the bond was never severed between us. For a number of years, we have both sought unsuccessfully to end our relationship. Whatever happens, this time, I know God is able. In the end, God will get the glory that's due His name. For now, I don't have to know how He will accomplish this. In the dark times, we have to remember the things that we believed in the light. All things are still working for my good.

Notes

Johnson, Henry Lee

STATE OF GEORGIA - PRIOR SENTENCES

CASE NO:	426503
OFFENSE:	FORGERY 1ST DEGREE
CONVICTION COUN-TY:	MUSCOGEE COUNTY
CRIME COMMIT DATE:	06/17/1999
SENTENCE LENGTH:	4 YEARS
CASE NO:	426503
OFFENSE:	ROBBERY
CONVICTION COUN-TY:	MUSCOGEE COUNTY
CRIME COMMIT DATE:	06/09/1999
SENTENCE LENGTH:	4 YEARS
CASE NO:	426503
OFFENSE:	THEFT BY SHOPLIFTING
CONVICTION COUN-TY:	COWETA COUNTY
CRIME COMMIT DATE:	04/08/1999
SENTENCE LENGTH:	5 YEARS
CASE NO:	426503
OFFENSE:	POSS OF COCAINE
CONVICTION COUN-TY:	MUSCOGEE COUNTY
CRIME COMMIT DATE:	11/05/1998
SENTENCE LENGTH:	2 YEARS
CASE NO:	426503
OFFENSE:	THEFT BY SHOPLIFTING
CONVICTION COUN-TY:	MUSCOGEE COUNTY
CRIME COMMIT DATE:	11/05/1998
SENTENCE LENGTH:	2 YEARS
CASE NO:	355337

OFFENSE:	CRIMINAL TRESPASSING
CONVICTION COUNTY:	MUSCOGEE COUNTY
CRIME COMMIT DATE:	07/05/1995
SENTENCE LENGTH:	12 MONTHS
CASE NO:	355337
OFFENSE:	THEFT BY SHOPLIFTING
CONVICTION COUNTY:	MUSCOGEE COUNTY
CRIME COMMIT DATE:	07/05/1995
SENTENCE LENGTH:	2 YEARS
CASE NO:	172735
OFFENSE:	POSS NARCOTICS OPIATES
CONVICTION COUNTY:	MUSCOGEE COUNTY
CRIME COMMIT DATE:	03/26/1989
SENTENCE LENGTH:	3 YEARS
CASE NO:	355337
OFFENSE:	POSS OF COCAINE
CONVICTION COUNTY:	MUSCOGEE COUNTY
CRIME COMMIT DATE:	03/26/1989
SENTENCE LENGTH:	2 YEARS
CASE NO:	172735
OFFENSE:	violation motor vehicle law
CONVICTION COUNTY:	MUSCOGEE COUNTY
CRIME COMMIT DATE:	03/26/1989
SENTENCE LENGTH:	12 MONTHS
CASE NO:	172735
OFFENSE:	OBSTR OF LAW ENF OFFICER
CONVICTION COUNTY:	MUSCOGEE COUNTY
CRIME COMMIT DATE:	03/26/1989
SENTENCE LENGTH:	3 YEARS
CASE NO:	355337

OFFENSE:	THEFT BY SHOPLIFTING
CONVICTION COUNTY:	MUSCOGEE COUNTY
CRIME COMMIT DATE:	09/20/1986
SENTENCE LENGTH:	10 YEARS
CASE NO:	172735
OFFENSE:	NOT AVAILABLE
CONVICTION COUNTY:	MUSCOGEE COUNTY
CRIME COMMIT DATE:	08/08/1984
SENTENCE LENGTH:	NOT AVAILABLE
CASE NO:	77516
OFFENSE:	S/D NARCOTICS OPIATES
CONVICTION COUNTY:	MUSCOGEE COUNTY
CRIME COMMIT DATE:	N/A
SENTENCE LENGTH:	6 YEARS
CASE NO:	77516
OFFENSE:	POSS NARCOTICS OPIATES
CONVICTION COUNTY:	MUSCOGEE COUNTY
CRIME COMMIT DATE:	N/A
SENTENCE LENGTH:	5 YEARS
CASE NO:	117352
OFFENSE:	ESCAPE
CONVICTION COUNTY:	MUSCOGEE COUNTY
CRIME COMMIT DATE:	N/A
SENTENCE LENGTH:	2 YEARS
CASE NO:	172735
OFFENSE:	POSS FIREARM CONVCT FELON
CONVICTION COUNTY:	MUSCOGEE COUNTY
CRIME COMMIT DATE:	N/A
SENTENCE LENGTH:	4 YEARS
CASE NO:	77516
OFFENSE:	BURGLARY

CONVICTION COUNTY:	MUSCOGEE COUNTY
CRIME COMMIT DATE:	N/A
SENTENCE LENGTH:	6 YEARS
CASE NO:	172735
OFFENSE:	THEFT BY SHOPLIFTING
CONVICTION COUNTY:	MUSCOGEE COUNTY
CRIME COMMIT DATE:	N/A
SENTENCE LENGTH:	4 YEARS
CASE NO:	172735
OFFENSE:	THEFT BY SHOPLIFTING
CONVICTION COUNTY:	MUSCOGEE COUNTY
SENTENCE LENGTH:	5 YEARS
CASE NO:	117352
OFFENSE:	THEFT BY SHOPLIFTING
CONVICTION COUNTY:	MUSCOGEE COUNTY
CRIME COMMIT DATE:	N/A
SENTENCE LENGTH:	6 YEARS
CASE NO:	77516
OFFENSE:	ROBBERY
CONVICTION COUNTY:	MUSCOGEE COUNTY
CRIME COMMIT DATE:	N/A
SENTENCE LENGTH:	6 YEARS

STATE OF GEORGIA - INCARCERATION HISTORY	
INCARCERATION BEGIN	INCARCERATION END
09/03/1999	10/01/2003
03/06/1996	07/04/1997
06/07/1991	02/25/1994
02/24/1987	11/01/1988
10/04/1984	05/14/1986
08/17/1983	12/06/1983
02/19/1979	01/19/1983
11/13/1973	06/13/1978

Johnson, Varetta Diane

STATE OF GEORGIA

INCARCERATION DETAILS	
MAJOR OFFENSE: FORGERY 1ST DEGREE	
MOST RECENT INSTITUTION: MILAN STATE PRISON (W)	
MAX POSSIBLE RELEASE DATE:	01/20/2005
TENTATIVE PAROLE MONTH:	08/1992
ACTUAL RELEASE DATE:	08/31/1992
CURRENT STATUS:	PAROLE
KNOWN ALIASES	
A.K.A. JOHNSON,LORETTA DIANE	
A.K.A. JOHNSON,VORETTA DIANE	
A.K.A. JOHNSON,WARETTA DIANE	
A.K.A. JONES,DEBRA	
A.K.A. WILLIAMS,VARETTA	
A.K.A. WILLIAMS,VARETTA DIANE	

CASE NO:	286122
OFFENSE:	THEFT BY SHOPLIFTING
CONVICTION COUNTY:	COBB COUNTY
CRIME COMMIT DATE:	06/30/1991
SENTENCE LENGTH:	3 YEARS
CASE NO:	286122
OFFENSE:	FORGERY 1ST DEGREE
CONVICTION COUNTY:	COBB COUNTY
CRIME COMMIT DATE:	06/30/1991
SENTENCE LENGTH:	3 YEARS
CASE NO:	286122
OFFENSE:	THEFT BY SHOPLIFTING
CONVICTION COUNTY:	CLAYTON COUNTY
CRIME COMMIT DATE:	06/04/1991

SENTENCE LENGTH:	5 YEARS
CASE NO:	286122
OFFENSE:	THEFT BY SHOPLIFTING
CONVICTION COUNTY:	CLAYTON COUNTY
CRIME COMMIT DATE:	09/12/1990
SENTENCE LENGTH:	5 YEARS
STATE OF GEORGIA - PRIOR SENTENCES	
CASE NO:	220511
OFFENSE:	THEFT BY TAKING
CONVICTION COUNTY:	DEKALB COUNTY
CRIME COMMIT DATE:	06/29/1987
SENTENCE LENGTH:	2 YEARS
CASE NO:	220511
OFFENSE:	THEFT BY TAKING
CONVICTION COUNTY:	FULTON COUNTY
CRIME COMMIT DATE:	05/07/1987
SENTENCE LENGTH:	3 YEARS
CASE NO:	220511
OFFENSE:	conversion leased property <$101
CONVICTION COUNTY:	FULTON COUNTY
CRIME COMMIT DATE:	04/30/1985
SENTENCE LENGTH:	3 YEARS
STATE OF GEORGIA - INCARCERATION HISTORY	
INCARCERATION BEGIN	INCARCERATION END
10/21/1991	08/31/1992
05/19/1988	02/23/1989

Russell, Charlotte

MAX POSSIBLE RELEASE DATE:	08/29/1996
TENTATIVE PAROLE MONTH:	08/1987
ACTUAL RELEASE DATE:	08/01/1987
CURRENT STATUS:	INACTIVE

KNOWN ALIASES
A.K.A. HALL,CHARLOTTE RUSSELL
A.K.A. RUSSELL,CHARLOTTE A
A.K.A. RUSSELL,CHARLOTTE ANITA

STATE OF GEORGIA - CURRENT SENTENCES	
CASE NO:	198279
OFFENSE:	POSS NARCOTICS OPIATES
CONVICTION COUNTY:	MUSCOGEE COUNTY
CRIME COMMIT DATE:	04/15/1986
SENTENCE LENGTH:	10 YEARS
CASE NO:	198279
OFFENSE:	POSS OF MARIJUANA
CONVICTION COUNTY:	MUSCOGEE COUNTY
CRIME COMMIT DATE:	04/15/1986
SENTENCE LENGTH:	10 YEARS
STATE OF GEORGIA - INCARCERATION HISTORY	
INCARCERATION BEGIN	INCARCERATION END
10/30/1986	08/01/1987

Other Titles

By

Dr. Charlotte Russell Johnson

A Journey to Hell & Back
ISBN 0974189308

Daddy's Hugs
ISBN 0974189316

The Flip Side
ISBN 0974189324

Grace Under Fire
ISBN 0974189332

Mama May I
ISBN 0974179340

Mama's Pearls
ISBN 0974189359

Kissin' Hell Goodbye
ISBN 0974189375

Breaking the Curse
ISBN 0974189369

Reaching Beyond, Inc.

www.charlotterjohnson.com

Helping hurting humanity to reach beyond the barriers in their life, one barrier at a time.

ORDER FORM

Know someone else in crisis, or in need of encouragement order additional copies of this book to sow seeds of healing grace.

Postal Orders:

Reaching Beyond, Inc.
P. O. Box 12364
Columbus, GA 31917-2364
(706) 573-5942
Email us at: admin@charlotterjohnson.com
Please send the following book(s).

Qty.	Title	
_______	*A Journey to Hell and Back*	$14.95 each
_______	*The Flip Side*	$15.95 each
_______	*Daddy's Hugs*	$12.95 each
_______	*Grace Under Fire*	$14.95 each
_______	*Mama May I*	$14.95 each
_______	*Mama's Pearls*	$14.95 each
_______	*Breaking the Curse*	$14.95 each
_______	*Kissin' Hell Goodbye*	$14.95 each

Sales tax:
Please add 7% for books shipped to GA addresses.
Shipment:
Book rate $3.50 for the first book and $1.50 for each additional book.

Also available at www.charlotterjohnson.com

www.ingramcontent.com/pod-product-compliance
Lightning Source LLC
La Vergne TN
LVHW050620100826
845148LV00011B/1668

* 9 7 8 0 9 7 4 1 8 9 3 4 5 *

www.ingramcontent.com/pod-product-compliance
Lightning Source LLC
LaVergne TN
LVHW050620100826
845148LV00011B/1668

* 9 7 8 0 9 7 4 1 8 9 3 4 5 *